a girl called karen

a girl called karen

A True Story of Sex Abuse and Resilience

KAREN McCONNELL
WITH EILEEN BRAND

JOHN BLAKE

Published by John Blake Publishing Ltd,
3 Bramber Court, 2 Bramber Road,
London W14 9PB, England

www.blake.co.uk

First published in hardback in the UK in 2006

ISBN 1 84454 234 3

British Library Cataloguing-in-Publication Data:

A catalogue record for this book is available from the British Library

Design by www.envydesign.co.uk

Printed in Great Britain by Creative Print & Design

1 3 5 7 9 10 8 6 4 2

Papers used by John Blake Publishing are natural, recyclable
products made from wood grown in sustainable forests.
The manufacturing processes conform to the environmental
regulations of the country of origin.

Every attempt has been made to contact the relevant copyright-holders,
but some were unobtainable. We would be grateful if the appropriate people
could contact us.

Contents

Acknowledgements

For their contributions to my growth as a human being and a social worker, I thank Dr. David Harrison, who shaped my understanding of good social work; Mary Groff, who influenced me to go to school; and Shelia Myrick, who showed me by example what real social work is. For their interest, advice, and encouragement, I thank my US publisher, Lyle Stuart, editor Sandra Lee Stuart, and the entire staff of Barricade Books, who demonstrate immeasurable skill and patience.

Prologue

In 1998, two years after I earned a master's degree in social work from the University of Alabama, the Board of Directors of Tennessee Valley Family Services in Marshall County, Alabama, offered me a position as executive director of the agency. It felt as if my whole life had led to that place and that job.

My first experience with the foster care system began when I was twelve. I spent my teen years growing up in a foster home where I had been placed by Catholic Charities. Later in life, my husband, Russ, and I volunteered to foster teens. In fact, two of our foster daughters were residents of the agency's shelter program before they came to live with us.

I also had experience on the other side of the fence. I had worked for more than four years as a caseworker for children and family services in the state system. During those years, I was often at Ogden House, the shelter program operated by Tennessee Valley Family Services, dropping off or picking up young people.

When the state hired me to work with children in 1990, my primary qualifications were my education and experience in writing and executing training programs. I implemented an innovative program for foster children in need of therapy. I recruited and trained families to provide specialized care for difficult children. It was then my responsibility to evaluate, place, and supervise the treatment of foster children with a dual diagnosis of emotional, mental, or physical problems. It was exciting, challenging, and stressful.

The longer I worked, the more I recognized that I did not have a solid educational background for working in this area. That's when I returned to school to become a better social worker.

When I accepted the responsibility of directing the business of Tennessee Valley Family Services, I was faced with two dilemmas. First the local schools had a territorial dispute about whose responsibility it was to educate the youth who came to Ogden House. The board of directors and my predecessor had tried to resolve the issue for more than two years. They had been able to negotiate a temporary reprieve for the school year prior to my arrival. Now the issue was at hand.

Then Morris Dees's Southern Poverty Law Center filed suit in my name as the friend of a young black foster child who was denied access to two local high schools. It was a scary time. All the major state newspapers and some national publications carried stories about the situation. The local television crew interviewed me, and the story went nationwide. I had not anticipated my fifteen minutes of fame, and it was useful but disconcerting.

The lead attorneys, Michael Cohen and Ellen Bowden, did an outstanding job of securing the educational rights of the children without offending the individual defendants. As is appropriate, the children who reside at Ogden House now go to school wherever it is in their best interest, and the staff members at Ogden House work very hard to cooperate with the schools.

Classroom teachers and local school administrators were always on our side. It was an issue of how funds are allocated that caused administrators to resist taking the children. After the resolution of the suit, there was no animosity on the part of the educators, and I felt the resolution was amicable.

Now I had to turn my attention to our second dilemma. Our licensing agency had made it very clear that the existing shelter was not up to the revised standards for residential facilities. We had been grandfathered in, but that could not continue indefinitely.

In 1999, I began the journey to build a new home. First, I did a lot of research about structures and the cost of construction. As I prepared to kick off a fund-raising campaign, I received an anonymous donation of $40,000 from a family in the community. The check came in the mail at Christmastime. I was ecstatic. That gift made everything that came afterward possible. It gave me the confidence to pursue the dream.

We found seventeen affordable acres of land within the city limits next to a mobile home park. We made an offer and went before the city building committee to secure a permit to build. There we ran into difficulties. More than sixty people from the neighborhood showed up to challenge us. What we heard over and over again was that we did good work, but they did not want the facility in their neighborhood.

I was attacked personally, and it felt like a mob assaulting me. The building committee turned us down, although according to federal law, they had no right to deny us a permit.

I did not want to go to court again, and I certainly did not want our young people exposed to those people and their animosity. Our children come to us damaged, and it seems very wrong to contribute further to their pain. One older man at the meeting said that he had worked as an engineer, and he promised that he would "dog [us] every step of the way." I walked away from that meeting a smarter, though less trusting, woman.

With the help of a local family, we ultimately

secured thirty-two acres out in the country. It is a beautiful parcel of property with many options for future growth.

We had a kick-off event and started looking for contributions. During this time, I made two trips to Washington, D.C., to visit with our elected officials and make a plea for funds.

I met with the chief of staff for Richard Shelby, the senator from the state of Alabama. The first time we met, the young staffer was polite but not very encouraging. He was an attractive, courteous young man and the first-time father of an infant. He seemed not to be overly interested in the plight of our homeless youth.

The following year, I met with the same young man, who now had a toddler in the home. He had many parenting questions and expressed greater interest in the issues facing young people in our country.

Six months later, I received a call from the local office of Senator Shelby informing me that we were to receive $573,000 to build the new shelter. I screamed in delight.

The whole construction process was infinitely more complicated than I had ever imagined. Starting with environmental surveys right on through the interior finishing, I learned more about the construction business than I'd ever wanted to know. Thank goodness, I had one very dedicated board member who helped me every step of the way.

The most devastating point in the process was when the bids were opened and the lowest bid was $200,000 higher than we anticipated or had money to cover. We gave up many of the finer amenities in order to get within striking distance. One of my board members bought and gave us a small home and four acres abutting our property to facilitate the access.

When we had to move our building plans into the countryside, we incurred close to $50,000 in additional expenses for providing utilities.

There were many challenges. I am, after all, a social worker, not a building project manager.

In March 2002, we moved into our new building. It looks like a home, not an institution. It has a great big front porch with wide-bottomed rockers. The rooms are bright and cheerful and welcoming. No brick walls or tile floors. It is a home.

At the agency's annual dinner in October 2002, the Board of Directors of Tennessee Valley Family Services presented me with the template of a bronze plaque that reads, "This is the house that Karen built."

Today the plaque is mounted above the fireplace so that everyone who enters the home can see it.

The "house" symbolizes my life up till now – that unique structure with its secret rooms and closets, its tremendous family room, the narrow twisty staircase with its half-built safety rail and almost-safe landing, the rooms for learning and growing, the sociable veranda that's great for people watching and neighboring, the long corridors that don't go much of anywhere, and the capacious kitchen with the counter that sweeps like a stage across the family room.

What an incredible array of events has taken place in my time on earth! That evening when my board of directors recognized my achievements by unveiling the bronze plaque may well have been the highlight of my professional career. It capped a life that ran the gamut from an idyllic early childhood to the shocks of sexual abuse and desertion to acquiring skills of resiliency.

I have given birth to three children, accumulated three more through marriage, and nurtured two foster children. They have produced eleven beautiful grandchildren. Only two actually carry my DNA, but they are all my grandchildren.

Long after my children were born, I got a B.A. and eventually my master's in social work. I moved from taking in people's ironing to becoming the first woman supervisor in a cake-mix factory to surviving the emotional stresses of a dedicated social worker.

This book is rich with case histories culled from my professional colleagues and my observations and studies in my chosen field.

You could say that these life experiences, good and bad, have offered diversity so unusual as to enliven and authenticate my observations. I have written as candidly as I could, mistakes and all, though no tome could be big enough to include all of my blunders.

I have told my story because I think it illustrates some of the most important skills embodied in resilience. There are people who come by it almost instinctively, like the young book publisher who was frustrated by his company's profit-and-loss statement. So he canceled his appointments, left his ever-ringing phones, walked across the street, and sat alone quietly on a park bench for two hours. When he went back to the office, he put changes into effect that transformed his struggling young business into a thriving, growing, prosperous company that became a legend in the publishing world.

There was nothing magical about it. He had simply stopped viewing publishing as it had been traditionally conducted. He took a long hard look at each of the operations of his company, studied them in a new way as if he had never considered them before. Without realizing it, he had used Element No. 7, the ability to reframe, which I have described in my chapter called "Capturing Resiliency." That's how he worked out a more efficient way of running his firm.

Other people have no idea what resiliency is, where to get it, or how to incorporate it into their daily lives.

But we can all learn. I was lucky enough to see how my accomplishments came about and how to keep building on successes as the years go by.

So can you. There are guidelines here.

I have identified in Part III the seven factors that contribute most to resilience, and I devoted an entire chapter to each component. I have observed from my research that these elements can be taught to adults and children alike. I recommend them to anyone who is searching for help in guiding young lives beyond tragic beginnings. And they are a wonderful aid to all those adults and adolescents who are looking for more and better choices in their own lifestyles.

I wrote this book especially for foster parents, therapists, social workers, child-care counselors, house parents, clergy, project counselors, law enforcement professionals, teachers, and all those men and women who care about our children and our civilization.

Does anyone need to be told that our young people are our future? Personal resilience and societal responsibility are yoked for the advancement of humankind.

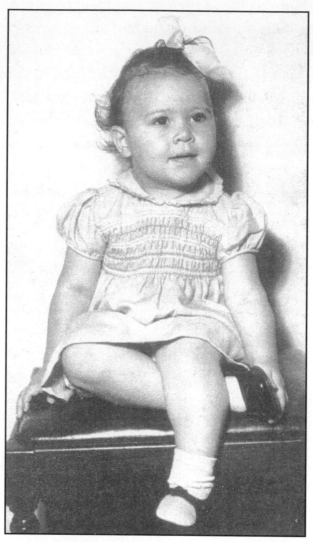

Two-year-old Karen sitting on her mother's sewing bench.

PART ONE

THE EARLY YEARS

CHAPTER ONE

That Awful Night

Sometimes when you bury things, the memory stays but details get lost. I'm not sure of the date or time of what I'm about to tell you, but I remember for sure every detail I've written here. And more besides. I'm certain no adult trauma or sophisticated inquiry or appalling case study will ever scrub the shock of that awful night from my mind.

I know that before it happened, I had been scared, and I wanted my mother. I was eleven at the very most. My mother was not there, and I went looking for her scent and the comfort of her place. It was late, and my father was not home when I curled up in my parents' bed. Sleep came quickly, deep and hard. Waking came gradually and in stages.

A hand was between my legs, touching, stroking, kneading. I froze. I didn't breathe or move or make the slightest sound. I felt funny in a pleasurable, scary kind of way. The hand kept touching me down there in the place my parents said I must never touch except for when I should wash myself in a hurry. The nuns at school said so, too, and they threatened us girls with eternal damnation if we let anyone put their hands Down There.

I knew I wanted that hand to stop, but I didn't want it to stop. Maybe, I thought, if I just take tiny breaths or don't breathe at all, this will turn out to be the weirdest, most shocking nightmare I ever had and I can forget all about it when I wake up. But even as I forced my breath into the littlest sighs, the hand went on roaming over my Secret Place, first lightly, then faster and more insistently, fondling and fingering, rubbing and circling until suddenly an invasive, brutal finger rammed into my flesh and plunged all the way inside me.

It was a real nightmare, it wasn't a dream.

I never knew you could shove something right into the flesh down there. I never knew there was an opening to a cave that could almost devour a rude exploring finger. I never even knew I had a hole down there.

I think now that things would have been bad enough if that had been the end of it. But my nightmare continued. There was so much I didn't know – much that I had to learn. As I thought about it all night long, I got more confused, more terrified. Maybe that was the way people got babies, I thought. Was I going to have a baby and be the shame of the whole neighborhood? I prayed I wouldn't get a baby. I prayed I wouldn't shame the neighborhood.

I loved my neighborhood. It was the best place, and my house was the best place, and I was the most important child in our home because I was the oldest and the best at taking care of my five young brothers and sisters. Everybody knew that.

Until that Awful Night, I thought my family was about like all the others on our street. True, our house was more rambunctious, bigger, shabbier, livelier, noisier; more alive with tears and laughter and songs and chatter and rivalries and squabbles. It was seldom empty – mostly full of people, very young people. When my mother's roses were in bloom, our yard was a riot of sensuous color, and they were the pride of our community. Otherwise our yard was the biggest mess in the neighborhood.

True, we had special perks. Even though Toledo was a long way from darkest Africa, because our father was the veterinarian for the zoo, our fun and games included free rides just about whenever we wanted them on a scruffy dusty camel or a gentle gray elephant called Toots. Those unusual privileges made us the envy of the neighborhood kids.

Our family was the largest on Algonquin Parkway. That's because my mother became pregnant eight times and gave birth to six babies in eleven years.

Keeping track of that heroic record, our priest gave joyful praise after every birth, and my Grandpa John (my father's father) snorted "no self-control" every time his son sent word that another one had arrived.

Whether my father was astonished or perturbed at such fecundity was never clear. He loved us kids very much, there was no question of that, and he worked endlessly with only a few interruptions to support the lively brood that he and Sally made.

CHAPTER TWO

The Parents
of My Parents

I was proud of my family, I was proud of my neighborhood, and I was proud of my ancestors, too.

My mother's family came to this country at the turn of the twentieth century. Her family was from somewhere in Eastern Europe, and they continued to speak to each other in the language of the old country.

Grandpa was from Poland. He died before I was born so I never knew him, and my information about him is very sketchy. I can tell you that he worked in the coal mines of Pennsylvania. There in the coal country, he met and married my grandmother. They moved to the Upper Peninsula of Michigan, and my grandfather acquired a lumber mill. Apparently he became fluent in English, worked extremely hard, did very well in business, and grew quite wealthy. In addition, he was active and influential in local politics. He fathered five children, one of whom was my mother, Sally.

He has been described as driven and intense. When the Great Depression drove him into bankruptcy and destroyed him financially, he committed suicide. I know only that he went into the woods and hanged himself from the branch of a sturdy tree. He had built his fortune from the forests, and that's where he ended his time on earth.

My mother told me very little of this tragedy, even though his disastrous end totally changed her life.

My grandmother never acknowledged it to me.

I loved my Little Grandma very much, but the language barrier made it difficult for us to communicate. When I was a young married woman, I brought Grandma to my home in Toledo for a visit. I invited a friend from my workplace who spoke Polish to talk to my grandmother and act as our translator. That's when I learned that, although my Polish grandfather spoke his native tongue fluently, my grandmother could not speak it at all. My friend said that Mary could mix some Polish in with English, but neither was her birth language. I tried to find out where she came from. I learned nothing conclusive, but I believe her family came from Hungary, and her native language was Hungarian. Obviously, my grandparents met and married without sharing a common language.

Parenthetically, I believe my grandmother's lack of

language and sophistication disturbed my mother when she was a young woman. As a child, I had observed the relationship between my mother and her mother. It was for my mother a mixture of love and frustration. For Little Grandma, it was a source of unstinting pride.

When my mother died, my grandmother's grief was inconsolable. This was the one child who'd stayed connected to her, and now she was gone. But that loss came years after grandpa's suicide abandoned Mary to the life of a poverty-stricken widow.

After grandfather's death, Grandma Mary continued to live in Iron Mountain, Michigan. It was a remote little place, and her children gradually left town. Finally, she was left with Alex, her youngest. There was speculation in my father's family that this child, who came much later than her first four children, might actually have been an illegitimate offspring of my mother Sally. I asked my grandmother about this, and she exploded. She never had learned much English, but there was no doubt that she was screaming that Alex was *her* baby and people had lied about her baby.

Alex was severely mentally retarded. When he was in his teens, he was taken from her custody by the authorities and placed in an institution a long way from home. According to eyewitnesses, she wailed and cried and struggled so hard to keep her baby, who was then about sixteen years old, that the police came close to locking her up. Finally she was forced to accept her loss, but she didn't forget Alex, and for years, she never failed to take the bus each month to visit him in the institution where he was confined.

Whether that heartbreaking experience served society well, I really don't know, but it took a cruel toll on my Grandma Mary. From then on, folks in Iron Mountain considered her a bit strange.

The whole town of Iron Mountain knew her as "Little Mary." She lived above a bar and restaurant. She had one room of her own and supported herself by cleaning rooms for all the elderly men who lived there. She never really learned to count, but she was very careful with her money. She scrimped and saved enough to pay for her funeral and burial arrangements when she died.

I visited Little Grandma when I was a teenager, and I became acutely aware of her unusual status in the town. For example, the cloistered convent allowed Mary access – a most extraordinary circumstance.

Several years before Mary's death, I was in the midst of major life changes and had moved to another address when it became evident to the townspeople that Mary would have to go to a home for old folks.

I didn't hear about it. No one in Iron Mountain knew how to reach me. Had I known, I would have done my best to rescue her, but, limited as my time and resources were in those days, I might have been unable to do as well as she and her friends did when they placed her in the home.

It was nothing fancy, that home, but fancy wasn't what she needed. It was an old house, and it boasted a staff of compassionate people. They let her clean the stairs and certain rooms. It was satisfying labor for her. She knew there was hard and useful work to be done, and it was her job to keep on contributing. She had to work because that is what people need to do.

Eventually I learned what had happened to her, and I went to see her in Iron Mountain. When I visited, she was proud to show me her room, but she was even prouder that her chores were important. She was a productive, contributing citizen even at her advanced age. (I never knew how old she was, nor did she. Based on my mother's age, I estimate she died in her mid-eighties.) I believe that she lived the balance of her life in comparative peace. Very likely, it was the best place for her to live out her days.

When she died, my Aunt Catherine and I received her few worldly possessions. I was amazed to see that gifts I had given her had been carefully preserved and had never been worn. What was even more disconcerting was finding gifts to my grandma from my mother, who by that time had been dead for more than twenty years.

As years went by, I learned that many elderly people save things for a future they don't have, for golden years they won't live to see. I hope grandma got pleasure keeping the trinkets we gave her.

Little Mary's life offers vivid lessons. An illiterate girl whose family had grown up somewhere in Europe, married a Polish immigrant (whose language she didn't know). He crossed half a continent and a mighty ocean to a country he had never seen where first he dug coal out of the ground and then owned a lumber mill and got rich and powerful until the Great Depression broke him and he killed himself. His widow had borne him five children, and (except for Alex) she raised them to adulthood.

Consider this: First, she had been poor, then rich, again poverty stricken, and finally ended her days as a cleaning woman who eked out enough from meager earnings to pay for her funeral and burial arrangements.

I learned a lot about resiliency from my Grandma Mary.

As contrasted with my mother's parents, who were fairly new arrivals in this country, my father's family had been here a long time. The ancestors of my paternal grandfather (Grandpa John) immigrated to this continent from Scotland and England in the mid-1600s, and the family of my maternal grandmother (Grandma Lucile) came here the following century from England and Germany. Many Midwestern farm families had similar backgrounds, and no one took any special pride in it. Mostly they laughed at the

Daughters of the American Revolution and the "blue bloods" who paraded their ancestry.

Grandpa John was not much for bragging about his forebears, and he grumped about a genealogical search financed by his sister (Great-Aunt) May: "She wasted her good money for that nonsense! It doesn't matter a hill of beans who your ancestors are. Just because you can trace them back a few hundred years doesn't mean they amounted to anything. What you are now and what you do now, that's what counts."

Sometimes Grandpa sounded like he'd rather not be linked to his ancestors – especially not to his father. Once a year, he would take his youngsters to spend an hour with the "Old Cuss" at his farm. Totally estranged from his tightwad father, he would sit in his Model-A Ford staring through the windshield until the visit ended and his children came back to the car bearing or wearing bizarre gifts.

One time Aunt Eileen had draped over her seven-year-old body a golden fox fur half as big as she was. The Old Cuss had trapped the fox and skinned it, tanned and lined the fur, and saved it as a gift for her annual visit. Aside from allowing a snapshot of the child wearing this amazing luxury item, her mother said there was no appropriate occasion for its display, but for years, it was one of the little girl's treasured possessions.

My father never mentioned the Old Cuss, and he didn't talk to us about his family tree. Only in recent years has our genealogy been perfunctorily circulated among the younger family members, most of whom seem to agree with Grandpa John that lineage doesn't matter a hoot.

In retrospect, though, I think the unsung family history helped shape my father's life.

Back in this country's early days, my father's ancestors were Quakers, believers in peace and simplicity, opponents of rituals – alien to a religion featuring Low Mass and High Mass, rosaries and confessions, incense and sacramental wine, priests and nuns, and the Pope in Rome.

In more recent years, the family felt the strong influence of the Shakers. That was because Grandpa John's mother, Grace, was an orphan who was raised by Shakers – a small sect that guaranteed its own demise by segregating the sexes and forbidding sexual intercourse. EVER. There were a few Shaker villages in the United States, but the unappealing Shaker program didn't really get off the ground, and its failure saved the human race from extinction by abstinence.

The one taboo the Catholics and Shakers shared was birth control, though for very different reasons.

The Shakers got new members by raising orphans and persuading them to stay as adults in the Shaker community. They also got a few adult recruits – usually abused wives running from sadistic husbands. Their rigid, repressed society was not congenial to my orphaned great-grandmother, and she left the Shaker Village as soon as she could.

Even though the Shakers preached that all sex was sin, she opted for marriage and children. Unfortunately, she chose a mean, hard-working, stingy farmer, and the rocky marriage of the miser and the waif produced three excellent, though inhibited, children – John, May, and Ona. The parents divorced as soon as their kids were grown.

Grandpa John's philosophy drew upon the sternest strictures of the Shakers and the Puritans of New England and forbade, with equal ferocity, sex, smoking, and drinking. With such a dark moral code, sacramental wine and tobacco and extramarital sex had to be the ultimate evils, and Grandpa's taboos were so unrealistic that his children sought a different set of values. Sometimes they made awful mistakes.

I believe his only son (my father) was a troubled man with respect to his sexuality, beginning in his teens, most certainly continuing through marriage and fatherhood, and probably all his life.

Grandpa John was not alone in his struggle for appropriate sexual mores. The twentieth century moved from Calvin and Luther and the Popes to Freud and eugenics and planned parenthood and the pill and the sexual revolution. Maybe some day we'll get it right, but I doubt it.

Along with its ban on sex, booze, and cigarettes, the family repressed emotionalism. Self-control was the rule. "Don't complain. Never cry" was the unspoken good-behavior code. Aunt Eileen said that one time Grandpa John was jauntily whistling "Yankee Doodle" as he came into the house from the barnyard. Something was wrong she knew, and, sure enough, his thumb had been torn halfway off in a farm accident. She said any time his voice was that carefully controlled, you could be pretty sure he had suffered a physical injury or was in some sort of danger.

Grandpa John's Quaker/Shaker heritage with its sexual taboos gathered fuel from his work. In addition to running a farm, he was a teacher and superintendent of country schools. It was almost as politically vulnerable an occupation as a rural minister's. His children learned the hard way, "Control yourself. Don't complain. Never cry."

Even down to my generation, I was taught to stay silent and hide my feelings when disaster struck. I remember that when a marriage was going sour and I didn't know why and I didn't know what to do, I didn't fight. I could only cling. And hurt.

Grandpa John and Grandma Lucile were strong, hard workers. As farmers and teachers, for many years, they worked at both occupations at the same time. Their work ethic was rock solid, and that's how they raised their children. Grandpa was very strict and seemed scary to me. He expected hard work, and his rule was law. That's what he had learned from the stingy old farmer and the industrious Shaker.

I remember my family's visits to my grand-parents in Florida when I was a child. My father always spent a good part of our vacation working on the ranch, mending fences and burning fields. Grandpa was the boss, and my daddy, the successful professional, obeyed him.

I adored Grandma Lucile. I always felt that I was a very special person when I was with her. She would take me to Catholic Church even though she was a Protestant and didn't like Catholicism very much. She enjoyed reading and respected my passion for books.

The last time I got to spend with her was during my fifteenth summer. We cooked and ate and played. She took me to the movies, and we saw *The Roots of Heaven*. The movie terrified me, and I couldn't sleep. She heard me tossing and came to my room and made everything all right. Grandma Lucile's loving, comforting words that night are among my fondest memories. Going back to a home where I didn't really belong was so bleak a prospect and my loneliness and the need for her were so intense that I cried all through Florida and Georgia on my way home to Toledo.

It was the last time I ever saw her alive.

CHAPTER THREE

My Parents

Grandma Lucile's father ran the country store and post office in Oregonia, Ohio (population 300). She was nineteen when she married Grandpa John, and their first child was my father. He was born in 1914 when "Spare the rod and spoil the child" was the maxim of the day. Grandpa John's parenting was modeled on his tyrannical father's and his Shaker-trained mother's teachings. Though he became less repressive as the family grew, he demanded that his firstborn be a model of good behavior.

My father was a painfully shy little fellow, and his life as a first-grader was a disaster. Almost every day, he would come home from school wet and smelly, and Grandpa in despair and disgust would whip him with his leather razor strop, while Grandma would sob helplessly, "Oh John, oh John."

Finally the terrified little boy who became my father told his parents why he wet himself at school: The older boys made fun of him when he went to the toilet, so he was too shy and ashamed to go there anymore.

As a nine-year-old, he liked to search out nests of hairless baby mice and squeeze them until the feces dropped out. Since the name of the game was to get rid of mice, not much notice was taken of this exercise in sadism.

By the time he was ten, he had learned that China was on the opposite side of the earth, and he thought it would be fast and easy to dig a hole right straight through to China. He and his little sister, Eileen, began to dig and had gotten six inches deep into their shortcut to the Orient when Eileen, who was barely six and new to the hoe, cut her foot, and the two kids tore across the pasture field to the house for first aid. Both were shrieking – she because it hurt, he because he always cried at the sight of blood.

Considering his blood terror, it was amazing that, upon his parents' prompting, he chose to become a veterinarian.

The two kids never did get to China, no doubt because it proved foolhardy to give Eileen a hoe.

There was a time when my father was in the eighth grade that the family lived in Columbus, Ohio, for a year. He had to wash the dishes each night and would carefully pull the blinds shut so his friends couldn't see him doing that sissy job.

Even when he went to high school, my father was bashful and withdrawn. Instead of going out into the school yard on his lunch break, he would stay in study hall reading the *Congressional Record*. His grades were excellent. His social graces didn't include talking very much, and he didn't seem interested in girls. He had the reputation of being an exceptionally well-behaved teenaged boy.

He was very much interested in sex, however. After I grew up, I found out that my Aunt Eileen had to battle her brother, my father, when she was about fourteen. They had gone on some mission on horseback in the woods and for some reason, had to get off the horses. First he tried to push her down, pointing to his bulging pants, and saying, "We could have a lot of fun." When that didn't work, he tried force. Fortunately she was a farm girl well muscled from heavy field work and serious basketball practice, and she fought him off. She made sure she was never alone with him again.

Then she learned from her little ten-year-old sister that their big brother was grabbing and prodding her in forbidden places, so she told their father what her brother had done. What I've heard is that Grandpa John explained to him, and emphasized with a bit of fisticuffs, that he would kill him if he didn't leave those girls alone, so he left those girls alone.

My father never had a public girlfriend until he became a veterinarian. He went with a librarian for a while, and then he met my mother.

I feel that I knew my mother best. I think she was beautiful. She had a flawless complexion. People on the street would stop her and compliment her. She had dark eyes and hair, a wonderful laugh, and a lovely speaking voice.

Delivering a baby every year or two caused her circumference to fluctuate wildly. When her weight was down, she had a great figure and was well endowed, but most of my memories are of an overweight woman who had just given birth or was about to give birth. I was the oldest. Her sixth baby was just eleven years younger than I. There were also the two miscarriages to sap her energies. Yet she always had time for us.

Sally talked a lot and loudly. Maybe that was so she could be heard over the hubbub of her children. She embroidered beautifully and was an excellent seamstress. I can't attest to the earlier years, but as I got older, I noted that none of her projects ever got completed.

For instance, two days before the annual veterinarians' picnic, mama decided to make matching dresses for her four little girls. I still remember how cute the dresses were and how people fussed over us. What no one knew was that there were no buttons or buttonholes and there never would be.

Mama would work like a mad fool to meet a deadline, and then she'd lose interest. Even as a child, I found this irritating.

The first home that I have any memory of was a place with stairs. I remember parading around in my Aunt Mary Louise's high heels. It was an apartment that my mama lived in, mostly alone, while my father fought in World War II.

My first really clear memories are after my father came home and we moved to the farm. We lived in a large garage that adjoined the foundation of what would become our house. My younger brother, Larry, and I were joined by a new baby, Sandra Lee. This was a good place for kids, but it must have been very difficult for my mother. The facilities were primitive. She bathed us, and presumably herself, in a big kitchen sink behind a curtain.

My father's large-animal practice was growing, and he farmed as well. A hayride when I was a kid meant riding in a wagon on a mountain of new-cut hay, not one of those manufactured events with scattered handfuls of hay in the bottom of a wagon filled with city kids. I have good memories of long carefree days, bare feet, and tomatoes picked and eaten in the same sun-drenched outdoors.

Our next home was in the back rooms of my father's animal hospital. After a short time there, we moved several blocks to what I'll always remember as my childhood home. It was a big two-story gray house in a nice neighborhood. Even fifty years later, it is still a nice neighborhood, though the house seems much smaller than I remember from my childhood.

Isn't it interesting how the palaces of our youth dwindle into cottages when we visit them as adults?

In the next few years, our family grew to six children. I was the oldest, then came Larry, Sandra, Patricia, Grace, and David. As an eighth-grade assignment, I was required to write my autobiography. I began it with the words, "There were six of us." I concluded with the words, "Now there is one."

My mama kept coming up with wild schemes to entertain her brood. We loved those circuses, but the neighbors must have lived in fear of the next extravaganza. One of mama's most memorable creations was a backyard pool constructed of sawhorses, old lumber, and a tarpaulin. Mama filled it with water, and we splashed and played and got unbelievably dirty from the old black tarp.

CHAPTER FOUR

Heartbreak

Then the good times were over. By the time I was ten years old, mama's life had become a nightmare, and she acted more and more strangely. She and my father were having problems that a little girl couldn't understand. He was never home. So his increased absenteeism didn't concern me, but it meant a lot of heartache for her. One time my mother picked up the phone extension and heard my father speaking with another woman. She made me listen, I don't know why. I suppose she wanted a witness.

Another time she loaded us children into the car, drove to a quiet residential street where we all sat with her for a long time, not knowing what we were waiting for. Then my father emerged from the house. He hugged and kissed a woman there. My mother cried for hours.

I know what infidelity is now, and I can feel my mother's terrible pain, but I didn't understand it then. Mama said the woman my father was seeing was named Lucile, the same as his mother. Mama found this particularly reprehensible, though I'm still not sure why this compounded the crime.

My mother became ill and then a lot sicker. She would get very flushed, and she couldn't breathe. When I came in from play, I might find her huddled on the couch, red and sweaty. I'd help her take off her bra, loosen her clothes, and lie back.

I was terrified over and over again. She told me she was going to die, and I got mad at her. Day after day as long as she was able, she would take us kids to the races and gamble. Day after day, she lost a lot of money. She said she had to get some money so she'd have something to leave us when she died. How could she say such a thing? She shouldn't say that. What was I supposed to do? I was just a little girl.

After her sixthborn David's arrival, she wrote to her mother-in-law, Grandma Lucile, that she had told my father he had to do something to stop the chain of pregnancies.

She told Grandma she was having terrible headaches. My father didn't act like she was sick. I was just a little girl. What was I supposed to do?

I know that there are a lot of books out there that describe terrible abuse and tragic lives. Mine was not like that. My mother thought I was great. She told me that I was great. But then she started forgetting me. I was a scrawny eleven-year-old. Normally I rode the school bus, but this particular day, I was supposed to wait for my mom to pick me up. All the other school kids had been picked up, and no one seemed to notice me sitting outside the school by myself. It got later and later, and I became more apprehensive, so I decided to walk the six miles home. I was mad. I rehearsed my angry attack. My mama was going to know how bad she was.

When I got home, I found she was really sick. She seemed to have no concept of time and was devastated that she had forgotten me. That was only the first time.

On another occasion, I got sick and asked to go to the one phone available to students. I called my mother and told her I was sick, but she failed to respond, and I soiled myself. It became a nightmarish pattern.

As the days melted into weeks and months, I became aware that my clothes weren't clean enough. I would hand-wash panties and socks and hang them in my room, but I couldn't figure out how to clean my outerwear. There was no one to ask. The family infrastructure was disintegrating, my mother was dying, and no one seemed to notice.

My father was more of an enigma to me than my mother. I thought he was incredibly handsome, which makes me a pretty normal little girl. As was the case in the 1950s in this country, he was the disciplinarian. I know that he was consistently stricter with Larry than with his daughters, following the pattern of Grandpa John and the Old Cuss. We were all terrified of the razor strop, but Larry was really the only one to feel the lash. Girls got spanked, but not with the strop.

We all felt that he favored Sandra, who went everywhere with him (except on his Lucile visits and sundry other adventures). Sandy was attractive, fearless, and precocious. I know that my parents had at least one heated talk about Sandra's favored position. Still, I was invulnerable. I was the oldest.

My father was committed to his veterinary practice. He preferred healing large animals to working in a small-animal clinic. He was the racetrack veterinarian, and he became the zoo doctor. I believe he had a reputation for being the best large-animal doctor in the county. He was respected for his very good work and high professional standards.

We were considered community leaders because of his unique position as a professional and because my mother and her gregarious nature had established their social position earlier in their marriage.

Sometimes my father took the older kids with him on his calls. I shudder to think what we looked like after my mother grew ill. We were ragtag, disheveled little urchins.

I was with my father the night a local horse breeder wanted him to perform a late-term abortion on a horse. I was too young to understand most of what transpired, but I know that my father was in a rage about something, and we were afraid.

Later I learned that the breeder wanted a life-threatening operation performed on his mare to get rid of a fetus that he'd lose money on. His intent was to breed her again soon so she could produce a profitable foal for him, and he was willing to risk his horse's life for that reason. For a veterinarian, the medical injunction about saving lives was nearly as strict as the Hippocratic oath. So my father was outraged.

I remember the night my father came home from the zoo after working nonstop for three days in a futile effort to save a giraffe. He was devastated by the animal's death, and he had fallen very sick with malaria. When he was stationed in the Philippines, he got malaria and amoebic dysentery, and he suffered ever afterward when his resistance went down.

My father was wounded in World War II. I don't know how he was injured, but among his uniforms and medals in the attic was what I believe to be a Purple Heart. He also brought back straw skirts and big straw hats. When I grew older, I got to take them to school for show and tell.

Most of my memories of my father are related to his career. I loved the zoo, and I got to spend a lot of time there. Because I was the doctor's daughter, I had access to behind-the-scenes dramas. When the mother lioness ate all her cubs save the one the handlers rescued, a prominent zoo supporter took the baby lion to care for. The little guy got pneumonia, and my father took him back to the zoo for euthanasia. When he told me he was going to put the cub to sleep because it had no chance and was going to die, I got so upset that my father let me take the baby home to nurse. I fed the sick little animal every two hours and mothered it right back to health.

Then they returned the cub to the influential family. I felt cheated. After all, I was the one who saved its life, but I didn't donate the large sums of money that the other family did, so I wasn't allowed to keep it.

It was one of my first lessons in the power of wealth and privilege. I still had a lot to learn about this world.

One of my greatest joys was to hold onto my father's hand as we walked down the street or into the animal hospital at the zoo. He worked hard for long hours, and he was not readily accessible to us kids.

He was a quiet man, and I treasured his rare words of praise. One of my happiest memories is of the time when he attended my first piano recital, and, although I had played wretchedly, he complimented me on my performance. He said something to the effect that I had the best stage presence of anyone in the entire program. I think his words helped me become a good public speaker in later life.

I loved my father, I almost worshiped him, and I was always a little in awe of him.

As I gradually awoke that awful, awful night, I felt someone crowding into me, hot and shoving. It was a man, a strange man . . . no, it was not a strange man. Incredibly, it was my father, but it was not my father, and he was acting weird, and he was touching me down there over and over again. It was my father, the stranger, who jammed his finger into the hole between my legs and was pushing and pulling it roughly inside me. The painful pleasurable sensations kept on and on, and I had trouble controlling my breathing. I knew it had to stop, and I knew I didn't dare act like anything had happened. It was bad, really bad. I knew I would be in trouble, or he would think it was okay, or he would want to do it again. Any way you looked at it, I was facing eternal damnation. And so was he.

I moaned and moved as if I were about to awaken. He rolled to the side of the bed and padded out of the room. I had loved my father dearly, I thought, but his behavior now was just disgusting. How could he do such a wicked thing? How dared he do that to me? How could he perform an evil act that he knew would send me straight to hell? I didn't sleep again that long, lonely night.

The next day, my father acted the way he always did, but I knew I would never trust him again.

Months packed with turmoil and upheaval went by before I told anyone about what happened that night.

I can't remember my father being around much when my mother was ill, though he may have been there. She got weaker. Her body retained lots of water, and she became very large. She couldn't walk anymore. My terror grew.

We kids tried to help her as much as we could. The day came when she fell to the floor and couldn't get up. Mama had to go to the hospital. Children were not permitted to visit.

She had only been in the hospital for a couple of days when my father came home and without preliminaries said, "Your mother is dead." I screamed at him and called him a liar.

I could not believe it. I had not believed her when she said she was going to die. I should have believed her. I had not been a good daughter, and now I was abandoned.

After she was gone, the medics said it was a brain tumor that killed her.

CHAPTER FIVE

A Funeral and a Wedding

The next day saw a flurry of activity. One of the worst scenes took place at the family dining table. My father was eating supper with us, an event so out of the ordinary as to mark the seriousness of the situation. Little four-year-old Grace kept asking for her mother, and her father didn't answer. I finally shouted at Grace that her mother was dead, that she was gone and wouldn't be back.

My father began to weep. That was the most shocking thing that any of us had ever seen. I was so sorry that I had hurt him. All six of us were very still.

There was a funeral to prepare for. Some neighbors and people from our church came and did things for us. The older kids and the ragtag urchins were given haircuts and new clothes, and everyone could see how beautiful we all were.

A lady whose son was in my class at school came and took me shopping. She got me two of the most beautiful dresses. They weren't little-girl dresses, they were for a teenager and store bought. I was thrilled. I have never forgotten them, but I had very mixed feelings about this charity. It didn't feel right to have her buying things for me. We were not poor people. I believe she sensed my distress for she said that she had sons and had always wanted to shop for a girl. I accepted that explanation.

Other people brought food and flowers in abundance. I was pleased to realize they cared about us, but I wondered where they had been when my mother needed help.

Family came from far away. Everything that anyone said felt like criticism of my mother. She had died slow and hard, but no one seemed to understand that. My grief mingled with anger and gratitude. My Aunt Eileen was an anchor in the whole drama. She didn't make judgmental statements, at least none in front of me. She was available for comforting, and I think we all leaned on her. People from everywhere in northern Ohio came to pay their respects, and the funeral procession was lengthy. Then everyone went home, and somehow we were supposed to go on.

I should say almost everyone left – Grandma Lucile and Aunt Eileen and Aunt Mary Louise and Uncle Lyle stayed on and had supper with our family. Grandma Lucile and Grandpa John lived in Florida, and Uncle Lyle and Aunt Mary Louise lived in New York City, and Aunt Eileen lived in Chicago. Mostly everyone was pretty quiet, and then Uncle Lyle said to my father, "We know it's going to be awfully hard for you to manage with all these kids. We'd like to help.... Mary Louise and I want to take the two little ones to our home to live with us."

I held my breath. I knew that for me it would be unbearable to lose my little sister and brother, and they would be heartbroken to be separated from all of us and from each other. The six of us could hardly bear waiting for my father to answer.

"No," he said. "I want to hold my family together. I don't want to break us up. We can manage. We'll find a way to manage."

You could feel the sighs of relief all around the table. We were going to stay together and live with our daddy.

My girlfriends were my greatest source of comfort through the next days. My best friends were Gloria Rutkowski, Kathy Horton, and Carol Hill, and their mothers were quietly present in my life. I can't honestly remember any dramatic conversations or tearful scenes, but I did know they cared. I was a Girl Scout, and that was a comforting place to be. My Catholic school was my safe haven from all the hurts.

Mama had died in March, and somehow we muddled along without her. We were a family. We knew we had to stay together, but we argued and scuffled the way most kids do.

Shortly after mama died, Larry was given a gasoline-powered airplane. He loved it, and it was shattered when I inadvertently stepped on it. He broke into tears, and he chased me all over the house and the yard. He was beet red, sobbing, tears streaming down his face. I had never seen my brother like that, and I really thought he would kill me if he caught me. I think his profound grief for the loss of our mother spilled over that day.

Father hired a housekeeper to take care of the home and his children. I discovered that the woman was sleeping with my father in my mother's place, and I hated her. I was the leader, I was mean, and my siblings and I made her life miserable. In retrospect, it was one of the larger mistakes of my life. She genuinely liked us kids and probably would have made a compassionate stepmother, though I doubt that my father would have thought her a suitable wife. My father's relationship with her had developed too soon after mama died for us to accept her, let alone welcome her.

One day Larry and I, with some neighbor kids, got into an exciting fight with water guns. Our housekeeper tried to move the action out of the house. I defied her, locked myself in the upstairs bathroom, and dumped water out of the bathroom window so it whooshed through the kitchen window below, soaking the poor woman and the kitchen floor. She was one unhappy camper. I still refused to come out of the bathroom.

When my father came home, I was wrathful because of his betrayal of my mother's memory, and my rage grew greater as I remembered his sneaky midnight violation of my body. So I was sassy, and I ended my outburst by screaming, "And that woman has no right to be in my mother's bed."

He slapped me across the face.

First I had lost my mother, and now I had lost my father.

We six kids escalated the battle to rid ourselves of the housekeeper, and that "menace" soon went away and stayed away. Not long after that, father began seeing Marge, whom he said he met at a church function.

How can I describe Marge? It's difficult because my contact with her was so brief that it left me with few memories. I remember a skinny, short-haired blonde with bony feet and without much bosom. My mother was dark-haired with an ample bosom, just right for comforting little people.

We went to the drive-in movies one evening. Larry and Sandy and Patti and Grace and David and I sat in my father's car, and he sat in Marge's car. Other than that adventure in togetherness, we saw very little of Marge and did almost nothing with her. We never shared a meal. The two adults spent more and more time together. Eventually, we six kids were left with a housekeeper while my father and Marge went to Florida. I don't know where her six-year-old son stayed, but it was not with us.

They came home from their Florida vacation and walked onto our porch, looking tanned and affluent. They were surrounded by six excited, messy children bubbling over with delight because their daddy was home. We were together again. We needed to be a family. We *were* a family. But our delight wasn't reciprocated, our joy wasn't rewarded by hugs or kisses or any show of affection at all.

The vacationers never entered our house that evening. They didn't treat it as their home. They never seemed to realize we were not just a bunch of waifs. They never acted as if we were a family – *their family.*

Finally we calmed down enough and quieted our welcoming hubbub so they could make themselves heard, and, without bothering with any preliminary explanation at all, they abruptly told us they were married. MARRIED! I don't know which of them said it first.

I was stunned, speechless, in shock. I don't remember much. I don't remember what the other kids said, and I have no idea how long the honeymooners stayed. I never said any of the "right things," although in retrospect, I can't imagine what would be a right thing in that circumstance.

When I saw they were about to leave, I asked if they would be picking us up for church in the morning. My father looked at the ground and was silent. Marge said they had decided that we would not be attending church anymore.

That bombshell was yet more shocking than their marriage announcement. It was mean. It was cruel. It was disastrous.

What was I to do? I looked straight at my father and asked, "What about Catholic school?" He looked away. Marge said, "You will not be attending Catholic school."

I was dumb, mute, utterly shattered. Never had I contemplated the powerlessness of a child.

Don't whine, don't cry! I got a ride with parish friends to church the next morning, and I choked back my sobs as I told the priest I didn't know if I would ever be returning.

If you understand anything about Catholicism and especially twelve-year-old Catholic girls, you will know that I was totally involved with my religion. I attended a Catholic school, where the nuns were my strongest role models. My mother had died a very few months ago. The faith that we shared was my greatest comfort, and now I had been deprived of it.

Later on, my father and his bride said they were making living arrangements for all of us. They talked of buying an unoccupied estate, which included quite a bit of property, several stables, and two houses. My father and Marge, with her son, would reside in the main house, while Sally's six children would live in the servants' house with a housekeeper.

That plan offered hope. We'd get to see our daddy

and spend time with him, and his new wife couldn't help loving us as soon as she got to know us. So the kids all began their happy chatter about "when our daddy gets our farm."

My mother had died in March 1955. My father and Marge had been married in early summer, and I don't know exactly what happened next in the adult world. I only know that my sister Sandra and I were sent to New York in July for a "vacation."

We couldn't help looking forward to the trip. It was exciting to think of seeing the big city, and it would be wonderful to come back home to our family and our new home on our farm. So Sandy and I happily said goodbye to Larry and Patti and Grace and David and to my father, who was strangely very quiet. Little sister Grace had turned five in May, and David would be "tore" (four years old) in October.

All of us kids – even the little ones – were thrilled because we'd soon be back together again in a joyous reunion on our daddy's new farm.

CHAPTER SIX

New York

Sandy and I were visiting Aunt Mary Louise and Uncle Lyle in New York City. We thought almost everyone in New York was rich, but now I know that my aunt and uncle were not. They had lived in Hell's Kitchen in a cheap little apartment on Ninth Avenue where it got so hot on summer nights that sometimes they rode back and forth on the Staten Island ferry to cool off in the ocean breeze. They could ride all night for a nickel, and it was a way to keep cool. They had been living on money from the occasional odd job while Uncle Lyle was writing books and articles.

Their fortunes had now improved enough that they lived in a one-bedroom apartment in Manhattan's Greenwich Village. It was a nice place. Aunt Mary Louise was a neatnik and took pride in her house. It must have been tough for her to see her living room torn up night after night as we brought out our bedclothes and made up the living room couch before we settled down to sleep.

Sandy and I at ages eight and twelve had no clue to the sacrifice and generosity of that young couple when they housed and entertained us in the bustling overcrowded city.

The time in New York was a jumble of pleasure and pain. The city was exciting. I fell in love with Joe Whalen, one of my uncle's friends. He was my first crush, and I have remembered him my whole life.

Uncle Lyle could be wonderfully creative. One of my best memories is the subway play. We concocted a play and presented it to a captive audience while hurtling through the under-ground world of Manhattan. And our audience applauded us. One lady leaned in, clapped enthusiastically, and said we were pretty and talented. Others began talking, agreed we were very good, and offered to share snacks.

The whole experience was so affirming that I believe it contributed to my belief that I was talented. People say that New Yorkers are cold and unfriendly. I have never found it so. This rich experience set the stage for all my adult visits to New York.

Sandra and I loved going to the movie theater, which became the site of my first social protest. Because I was twelve, I was required to purchase an adult ticket at the higher price, but Sandy and I were directed to the children's section. It was filled with loud, sloppy kids, and I didn't think it was right for us to be seated there. I knew an adult was permitted to take a child into the quiet adult section, and I had bought and paid for an adult ticket.

I screwed up my courage and went back to the usher, to whom I explained the injustice of this situation. I was very scared when I did that, as I had been thoroughly indoctrinated in the belief that adults were not to be questioned. The usher was a great tall black man in an impressive uniform. He listened patiently, nodded his head slowly, and, behold, we were shown to the adult section.

We returned often, and he always gravely showed us to the adult section.

I credit my Uncle Lyle with encouraging this protest and my future social protests. My Uncle Lyle and later Aunt Eileen were instrumental in shaping my world view.

It was a great vacation, but it was marred by our differences in religious belief. Uncle Lyle was a card-carrying atheist, or he could have been if atheists carried cards. I, on the other hand, was a well-indoctrinated little Roman Catholic prepubescent female. It was the worst possible combination of self-righteous zealots locked in acrimonious combat.

Until this time, I had not encountered atheism. I had a vague idea that it was the lack of something. You know, like not believing in something. It had never occurred to me that someone could be more fanatic about denouncing religion than a missionary could be eloquent about an evangelical cause.

Catholics were still forbidden to eat meat on Friday. On one occasion, Uncle Lyle and his friend, Bill Gaines, the publisher of *Mad* magazine, drove to a frankfurter joint for Friday night supper. Little sister acquiesced very quickly to a juicy hot dog, but I was steadfast in my faith. I ate no supper that night. And I told Sandy she would go to hell.

Some of the religious discussion occurred after Sandra and I had gone to bed for the night on the living-room couch. Uncle Lyle would pull up a chair to ridicule Catholicism and preach atheism. I would often escape into sleep, leaving my eight-year-old sister to defend the faith against the infidel. Night after night, the logical adult would win the debate.

It was fun to visit New York, but these ongoing ecclesiastical discussions upset me. I identified my church with my dead mother and felt I must defend it at any cost.

Then a telephone call came from my father to Aunt Mary Louise. He asked her if she'd like to "try us" for a while.

I heard her explain this to Uncle Lyle. "I don't know what's going on," she said, "but it sounds as though he's not eager for their return."

Uncle Lyle was silent.

There was a second call the next day. Uncle Lyle

spoke with him, then turned to the three of us and said, "He's planning to give away five of the children."

He handed me the phone, telling me that I should talk with my father. I had just seen a movie in which the leading lady was a feisty, dramatic woman who had captivated the hero with her lively ways. So with this cinematic heroine as my role model, I dramatically denounced my father for his outrageous plan. I asked if "that woman" was still going to be with him. It was she who had said we would not be going to church anymore. It was she who had said, "You will not be attending Catholic school anymore." It was she who was making my father arrive at all those bad decisions.

That ended the discussion. My father refused to go on talking to me. I had no idea then that it would be the last time in my life that he would ever speak to me. Or that it would be the last time in my life that I ever spoke to him.

Uncle Lyle and Aunt Mary Louise had been startled by my father's request. Now Lyle was upset by my behavior. He said I should have been tearful and loving instead of snotty. Looking back though, I doubt that my attitude made much difference in the grand plans of the honeymooners. In any case, twelve-year-olds are not recognized for their diplomacy. A temper outburst was a rare response to conflict from me. The alternative I had found for "Don't whine, don't cry" was more often that I would simply withdraw.

I wanted to go home. I had been planning to go home. I knew I was needed there. I wanted my mother and my home and my church. I called my mother's best friend, Mrs. Smith, and she said that I could come to live with her. She would meet me at the airport.

Uncle Lyle bought me a plane ticket. He was annoyed at my father for not buying my plane ticket. I don't think Uncle Lyle had a lot of money, and he and Aunt Mary Louise were expecting their first child. A plane ticket for an ungrateful guest was not in his budget. I was really too young then to understand all this. As I grew older, I began to connect the dots.

So it was decided. My sister and I would be going home the next day. Aunt Mary Louise told us that we were welcome to stay in New York until things got straightened out. I would have none of it.

That evening Sandra walked into the bed-room where Uncle Lyle was resting on the bed.

Sandy had a lisp. Sandy still has a bit of a lisp. On this occasion, she said, "Uncle Lyle, can I talk to you?"

He sat up, surprised. Until this moment, Sandy had always been in my shadow.

"Can I tell you a secret?" she asked.

"Sure. What is it?"

"I want to stay with you."

Almost as a reflex, he asked, "But honey, what about your church?"

"Uncle Lyle, could I tell you another secret?"

"Tell me."

With some vehemence, she announced, "The Catholic Church has almost ruined my life!"

All of this was reported to me later. I saw Uncle Lyle coming from the bedroom. He went into the kitchen where Aunt Mary Louise was preparing supper.

"Guess what?" he said. "Sandy wants to stay with us."

"How do you feel about it?" she asked hesitantly.

"I'd love it!" he said. "You know I love both the kids."

"Let's talk to Karen," she said.

They called me to the dining table. They sat across from each other. Sandy sat at one end and I at the other.

Mary Louise spoke. "Karen, you know Uncle Lyle and I would be happy to care for both of you," she said. "I would see that you go to your church on Sunday, but I wouldn't avoid meat on Friday. We would work things out."

Then Uncle Lyle spoke up. "Sandy wants to stay with us," he said quietly. "We'd be happy if you – "

I interrupted him by speaking directly to Sandra Lee. "What about the church?"

She shouted at me: "The church has almost ruined my life."

I stared at her in disbelief. During the next twenty-four hours before my departure, I didn't speak another word to her.

So I went home, and Sandra stayed. For years, I felt that I had abandoned her.

CHAPTER SEVEN

First There Were Six and Then There Was One

When I got back to Toledo, I found that I had no family there. *Not a single one!* Every member of my family had disappeared. There was no big farm, my father and stepmother were gone, Larry and Patti and Grace and David were nowhere to be seen.

Mrs. Smith was waiting for me at the Toledo Airport, and she took me home with her. Hers was a great big noisy Italian household. The Smiths had five children, lots of pets, and a constant flow of extended family. I just slipped in and hoped that no one would notice I was there.

In bits and pieces, I learned what had happened to my family. I know that my father had been fired from his job as veterinarian at the Toledo Zoo. I know that the community outrage at his behavior was at fever pitch – especially among the Catholic parishioners – so that his veterinary practice had died away, and that the honeymooners had moved to Louisiana.

I heard that there had even been bad talk about my mother – questions as to whether some of us were really his children. I can only imagine his shock when he discovered how my mother in her pathetic effort to "leave something" for her children had gambled away the family's savings at the racetrack.

I know also that he had systematically disposed of all his children.

Larry had gone to live with Grandpa John and Grandma Lucile. I have always wondered how my father explained to his sixty-five-year-old father why his bright and lively eleven-year-old son couldn't stay with him and his new bride.

Sandra was with Uncle Lyle and Aunt Mary Louise in New York.

Patti was sent to an orphanage, where she remained until she was adopted.

My father first sent the two little ones to my Great-Aunt May and Great-Grandma Grace in Detroit in the hope that they would adopt them, but Aunt May consulted social work professionals, and it was agreed by all that Aunt May and Grandma were too old to undertake such a long-term venture. Then my father and Marge went to Wyandotte and took the children away, as Aunt May wrote later, "We knew not where."

That child-disposal plan having failed, their daddy

put little five-year-old Grace and three-year-old David in an orphanage in a suburb of Toledo.

Aunt Eileen had been out of touch with her family, and she did not learn what had happened until the two little ones had been in the children's home for more than a month. She immediately called her brother to ask that she be allowed to raise the two children. He said he couldn't get the children from the home. She asked Uncle Lyle and Aunt Mary Louise to intervene, and Lyle was able through mysterious means to persuade my father that failure to accede immediately to Eileen's request would work greatly to his disadvantage.

So Larry was in Florida, Sandy was in New York, Patti was in an orphanage in the Toledo area, Grace and David were with Aunt Eileen in Chicago, and I was trying to keep anyone from noticing me at the home of the Smiths in Toledo.

Incredibly, all six of us kids didn't get together in one room again until some twenty years later when Grace and Phil got married in New York.

I thought I was getting away with hiding out at the Smiths until the day that Mr. McCarthy came to visit. He was a social worker with Catholic Charities, and I was one of "his children." It seems that Mrs. Smith had rheumatic fever, and her home was not appropriate for me. For the next few days, I was paralyzed with fear. Up to this point, I had the illusion of some control over my destiny. Suddenly, I had none.

The day came that I had to say farewell to the

Smiths and climb into Mr. McCarthy's automobile. We drove and we drove. My new family lived out in Sylvania. It's just a suburb of Toledo now, with an almost unbroken flow of contiguous neighborhoods. Back then, it was as if I was moving far away to a different town. It was one of the longest trips of my life. I didn't know what to expect or what it would look like. I felt totally vulnerable.

When we arrived, I was impressed by the house. It was a large ranch in the middle of a wooded area.

Everyone in my new foster family was lined up to meet me. There were Mike the father and his wife, Mary, and sons Michael and Patrick and daughter Kathy. I shared a room with Kathy, the boys' bedroom was next to the girls' room, and the master bedroom was at the other end of the house. In the backyard, there was an in-ground pool and bathhouse. It was a large spacious yard. I liked it very much. I also liked being able to walk out in the woods, where I would sit and read for hours.

I was scared to death of doing something wrong. I didn't know where I would have to go next. I had been abandoned, and I felt abandoned. My family was gone, and people could do whatever they wanted to me. I knew it was imperative that I be very good.

Several incidents stand out from the early days in foster care.

Sometime during the first month, Mike went out of town on business. The boy Michael and I were horsing around in the living room, and I went over backward in the recliner, putting a gouge in the wall. The following night, I visited my friend Maureen Mackley's house. I was depressed and anxious. I was convinced that Mike would send me away when he returned home. Maureen's mom finally got me to open up. I think she must have called my foster father because I was comforted and reassured that I was not going to be sent away.

Throughout the first months, I routinely hid food and saved money like a miser. You just can't trust grownups. I got through all the first holidays. Then on Easter Sunday, Michael threatened me with a BB gun, and I went flying through the house, threw myself on my bed, and lay there sobbing. Mary came in to find out what went so very wrong. I kept sobbing that I wanted to go home. She told me my home was gone.

That was the first day that I faced and accepted my separation and loneliness and abandonment.

Since I got to remain at the same school that I previously attended, I kept my friends, my teachers, and the familiarity of the physical plant. That continuity and the love and protection of the sisters of Notre Dame created a protective barrier against much of my pain.

I also had my best friends. It seems that very early I learned the value of strong female friendships. To this day, fifty-odd years later, after finding each other in the fifth grade, Kathleen Maier and I are still friends. We are separated by miles and get together only occasionally, but the bond remains strong. Kathleen knew my mother. We have a history.

Judy Moon and I became friends in the seventies and know everything about one another. Judy is my touchstone. She is whom I call at 3:00 A.M. because I can't breathe. We have raised a lot of hell together, and we are growing old together.

Mary Groff became my mentor and then my friend later in life. Those three are my closest, dearest pals. There are also Donna Farish and Linda Mosley and Carol Jean Exby and Rita Hayes.

I have my children, whom I love dearly, but these women are my family in a way that children can never be.

I felt that my foster mother was a cold, unaffectionate woman. I didn't think it was just her attitude toward me. I don't remember any affectionate play between her and her husband, Mike. She did express affection to her own children, and she did take excellent care of all of us. Her home was immaculate, our clothes were beautifully cared for, and she was a good cook who had a meal ready every evening for her household. In her own way, I suppose she loved her family. I know that she never loved me or even particularly liked me.

When Mike died, I attended the funeral with my husband, and she introduced me as "the little girl we got from Catholic Charities."

What joining this new foster family meant was that I acquired three more siblings. I was twelve, slightly older than Michael, so I became the eldest of the four of us. He and I were never close, but we were not at odds, either. He was an attractive boy who was a little bit self-centered. We played when I first joined the family, but as I entered adolescence, we grew apart.

Patrick was a wonderful, sunny child who resembled his father. Mike the father was a recovering alcoholic, and unfortunately, Patrick inherited this predisposition for alcoholism. He had his dad's wonderful, outgoing personality, but he died very young, probably as a result of abusing his body with alcohol.

Kathy and I shared a room. She was an adorable child and a pleasant roommate, even though I was six years older than she.

I felt it was good for me to have these foster siblings. I was accustomed to caring for younger brothers and sisters and expected to fill that role in my new family, but the first time my foster parents went out alone, they secured the services of a babysitter. I was outraged. In fact, logically or not, all these years later, I am still incredulous. I had taken care of my brothers and sisters for years, and I had already baby-sat outside my home. I was a professional babysitter. I did not need a babysitter.

Another issue was family outings. If I preferred not to go out with the family, they felt that I did not appreciate them, when the truth was that adolescents routinely seek some independence and solitude. Or at least that was part of the truth as far as I was concerned.

The other feature that took a good deal of getting used to was the eating habits of this family. Mary would often prepare three different meals to satisfy the palate of each family member. I, on the other hand, had come from an environment where you ate what was provided or did without. If there was something that you found really odious, you could pass on that item and eat whatever else there was. Meals back on Algonquin Parkway were not customized to fit individual tastes as they were in my new home. Fortunately! It would have been an endless task to fix special dishes for each of us six youngsters.

I saw and ate my first shrimp during this early period with my new family, and I quickly gained an appreciation for that particular delicacy. Big Mike said that I was developing expensive tastes, although I knew he really liked it that I loved the new delicacy. Mike and I enjoyed a kind of camaraderie. I cherished all the love I could get.

As far as my real family was concerned, I was utterly alone. I was needy, and I was powerless. Among my sisters, Sandra was nearest my age. I knew I could have been with Sandra and Aunt Mary Louise and Uncle Lyle if the religious difference hadn't been the great issue. Still, I felt some satisfaction because I had chosen not to betray my church and my mother. In any case, Sandy was lost to me now.

Aside from our doctrinal differences, Uncle Lyle and I had become close enough that I had told him of my father's disgusting invasion of my body. I expected some sort of an explosion, outrage that you could hear all the way to Toledo, and I felt puzzled and betrayed by what I considered Lyle's inaction.

I learned later that he used his knowledge as a powerful "persuader" of my father when it really counted, but at the time, Lyle merely questioned me closely several times as to whether I had told anyone else about the episode. And then he was quiet. With my twelve-year-old penchant for simplifying all complexities, I confirmed for myself that this was something I must not talk about, a secret that must be buried somewhere deep within me and never told. Adults, it seemed, could never be trusted.

Perhaps that explains why I was such fair game for Mike, my foster father. It was a pleasant day, the day it first began. I was thirteen, thin, certainly no Lolita, though I had big dark eyes and a chubby face. I was on the phone.

The phone was a sore point with me. One of the most disagreeable rules at my new home was the telephone limit. I was allowed five minutes and no more. In teen-talk, that would hardly get you past the amenities. I have to admit that I was always pushing the limit while I was glued to the phone in the little niche outside the kitchen and the den. Mike chose a peculiar way to deal with my disobedience.

On this particular day, everyone had gone out except Mike and me. I was on the phone. He came and stood beside me. Instead of telling me to end my chatter, he began to massage my arms and then my back. I was grateful for the rare affectionate gesture. I kept on talking. And talking. He continued to stroke my skin up and down my torso very gently. I began to feel paralyzed, and I didn't move. His hands slipped lower and touched my skinny behind softly, almost as if by accident. It made me feel funny.

He stopped the minute he heard Mary's car enter the driveway, so I knew immediately that this was a secret.

Every time my foster father and I were alone – and it seemed to happen a lot – he would touch me. His finger teased me for weeks before he put it inside me. His hands played with my little-girl nipples, making them hard and sore. I never said a word to him. I never acknowledged even to myself what was happening. Somehow I knew I should try to avoid him, but the day always arrived when we were alone, and I couldn't evade him.

I was a little girl in so many basic ways. I didn't have my first menstrual period until I was fifteen and only then did I begin to fill out. I loved to run and play, and I escaped constantly into books. I had good girlfriends.

But, along with the little-girl pursuits, there evolved the secret life. Mike never came into my room or into the bathroom. I was never denied personal space or privacy. The thing was that I was fair game in the public rooms of the household, and I just couldn't hide out forever.

I never seemed to figure out when Mike's probings and proddings and sexual caresses were going to happen. We never talked about it. I always stood motionless. Both of us remained silent. We never looked at each other's face.

Our relationship got terribly skewed. Sometimes I asked to do something or go somewhere that ordinarily would have been denied, and Mike would give me permission. Not always, but sometimes I'd get special treatment.

I developed a dislike for Mary. If she would love him and be good to him, he wouldn't bother me, I thought. If she were a good mother, she would protect me. I believed she knew what was going on and failed to intervene because it got her off the hook. Anyway this was all a great big secret in this devout household that had been entrusted by Catholic Charities with the upbringing of a bewildered adolescent girl whose mother had died unexpectedly, whose father had abandoned her and parceled out her five brothers and sisters all across the country.

As I got older, it got more complicated. I even started to date. So, on the one hand I was getting from church and school and "family" this grim and serious message about staying pure. No sex before marriage. On the other hand, I was being slowly and methodically sexualized.

One day I came out of my bedroom to find the kids gone and Mary working in the yard. Mike was watching TV in his pajama bottom and nothing else. He beckoned to me. I stood by his chair as he moved his hands up my legs to my panties. He put his hand inside my pants and fingered me. This went on for quite a while, and then he did a new thing. He opened his pajamas where men go to the bathroom and pulled out his penis. It was big and red, and it looked angry. He took my hand, and I resisted, but he guided it to his penis and made me touch it. I didn't look. I just touched.

I hated the den. That's where it usually happened. He came to the den one day when no one was around, and he motioned to me to stand in front of him. He pulled down my underwear so he could see my private parts. It was shocking and humiliating. I didn't even let my little foster sister see me naked. He studied my body for a long moment and then began the stroking and massaging and fingering with yet more intensity than usual. He took his penis out and put my hand on it. He told me to squeeze it, and I did.

Miraculously, no member of the family or any guests ever happened to interrupt one of those scenes in the den. And there were a great many of those sessions over the years. They went on and on until I began to date someone seriously.

Then he just stopped!

I have been asked why I obeyed him, why I
acquiesced to his ogling and fingering and poking and
prodding, why I didn't go to the nuns at school and the
priests at church for help. I suppose the reason was that
I desperately needed his good will. He was the only one
who was there. His wife disliked me. My father had
betrayed and abandoned me. In my childish way, I
believed my mother had deserted me by dying. What if
I lost Mike? Who in the world could I depend on?

I'd like to tell you that it was all over when I got a
serious boyfriend, but there was one more time. I was
nineteen, had been separated from my young
husband, and was staying in Florida with my Aunt
Eileen and my little sister, Grace, and my little
brother, David. My foster father came to see me while
on a business trip. He took my little brother and sister
and me out to dinner. He was so very kind to the little
kids. He got them great big ice-cream treats, and then
he took them home.

Mike never said where we were going, and I didn't
ask. He took me to his hotel room. We didn't speak. I
stood there just as mute and passive as I had been all
those times in his den. Silently, he undressed me,
looked his fill at my body, lowered me onto the bed,
entered me, and had a quick orgasm. It was dirty and
degrading and a doubly bitter experience because I
hadn't known how to make it not happen.

It is difficult for the independent woman I am today
to understand how the young woman I was then could

have been so passive. I buried that day like a dirty little secret for years.

One day during a counseling session, while listening to a woman who had survived multiple beatings in the hell that was her marriage, I finally came to terms with my own choices. Just as that woman had finally left her abuser, so did I, but long ago on that afternoon in Florida, I did what I had been conditioned to do.

Soon afterward, I returned to Toledo and to my husband.

Mike never bothered me again. He treated me as a daughter. He said that I would always be his daughter and that I would share equally with his other children. That, of course, was a fantasy. He died a few years later, and at the funeral, his family scarcely recognized me. Mary was barely civil, and the kids were wrapped in their own grief. "The little girl they got from Catholic Charities" didn't belong.

Among the mourners, there may have been women who provided Mike with sexual relief after those sessions of foreplay with me in his den. I can't remember when I first became aware of his infidelities, but I knew he had affairs.

I never hated Mike. He was not inherently an evil man. He was entrusted with fathering a young girl, and he violated that trust and did bad things. But he contributed greatly to his community. He was a leader in the Catholic diocese of Toledo. He was in Alcoholics Anonymous for years and helped many in their struggle for sobriety. When he died, the funeral home was crowded with people who Mary and the kids didn't know.

People came forward with the same story, told over and over again. Only the details varied. Mike helped people. This person would be dead except for Mike. This person had built a business because Mike had faith in him.

Would anyone have believed me if I had talked about this paragon's exploits with a teenage waif in his den?

Mike was not the stereotypical abuser inasmuch as he never tried to control my life or limit my freedom. Except for that one shameful secret, he pushed me to be the very best that I could possibly be.

Mike was intelligent. He was born to a poverty-ridden family in the hills of Kentucky. He personified the story of the poor mountain boy who carries his shoes to school so he won't wear them out. He was the first person in his family to become a university graduate. He was teaching at a college before he reached his twenty-first birthday. Mike was bright, charismatic, and charming. He went into sales and was very successful.

Mike respected my intelligence and ambition. He was always proud of my academic achievements, and he consistently encouraged me to grow. Even with all the bad stuff, there was this supportive male figure wrapped up in the same person, and it was a desperate time. I needed his good will and love terribly.

"The Six of Us" together again after 20 years.
(L to R) Larry, David, Grace, Karen, Pat, Sandy.

PART TWO

Learning and Getting Stronger

CHAPTER EIGHT

Marriage and Divorce

I was in a dreary waiting room filled with some of the good folks of Alabama. Years earlier, I had obtained a Social Security number, made a note of it, used it for decades, lost the card, and never noticed its absence. But to get a job in Alabama, I was told it was necessary to present an actual Social Security card not just a number, so I was in the Social Security Office of Albertville applying.

There were forms. I didn't need to fill them out, a clerk behind the barred window would see to it.

"Tell me your maiden name," she said.

"Karen Strawn," I said.

"Spell it, please."

"S-t-r-a-w-n," I said.

I was wearing a wedding ring. "Any other name?" she asked expectantly.

"Karen Mikolajczyk. M-i-k-o-l-a-j-c-z-y-k. That's Mick-o-wize-ik."

Now we had the attention of everyone in the room.

"Any other name?"

"Karen Skutt. S-k-u-t-t."

She wrote it down. "Any other name?"

"Karen McConnell. M-c- capital C-o-n-n-e-l-l."

I glanced over the room filled with rapt observers and said, reflectively, "It took me a long time to find a name I really liked."

The owner of the name I really liked was Russ McConnell, whom I began dating in 1978.

A very great deal had happened in the two decades between my days in the foster home and my happy marriage to Russ.

I met Nick when I was sixteen. He was my first love, and for me, it was true what they say about your first love. It doesn't last long. He didn't have a car, and he stopped calling after a few months. It was a sad time for me.

We got together again in my senior year.

Today, all these years later, I can still remember the bittersweet struggle. I had been living five years of foreplay. Nick touched me. He made my nipples hard. We were both in a state of constant arousal.

We would make pacts never to be alone together because we wanted to wait for marriage. We went to confession.

Came the day that I knew we were going to make love. I didn't want to do it in the backseat of an old car, so I arranged a rendezvous that offered a bed and privacy. I can't say it was the most satisfying experience of my life, but I think I never again felt so powerful. We dated for two years, we had to sneak around, the sexual tension was painful.

Marriage was nowhere in the offing, and, as time went by, I yearned for a home, marriage, and security so badly that I began to pull away.

By the time I completed high school, I had been babysitting and working at a drive-in long enough to have some savings. I bought a car and rented an apartment and moved out of my foster home. Mary made a terrible fuss, and I had to go back. It seemed foster children were required to live at "home" till they were eighteen.

I graduated with many honors, and I was offered a scholarship to a college in Toledo. The program offered there was deadly, and I dropped out in my first quarter.

Dick Mitchell came into my life with all the swashbuckling swagger of a newly discharged marine. He was handsome, and I was crazy about him. He had a married girlfriend named Sharon. He shamed me in many situations, but he married me. Just before we were married in 1961, his sister told me that their family name was Mikolajczyk, that it was Dick's legal name, and it was the name I would carry when I was married.

Dick and I had a classic fifties marriage for the first decade. He worked and ruled the roost. Sharon continued to run Dick's life in ways that humiliated me up to the day she died in her early thirties.

In some respects, the assault on my womanhood, which I had experienced as a foster child and before, continued into my marriage. It was not a physical assault, but rather an emotional deprivation. My young husband often withheld sex and affection. He was still incredibly attractive and charismatic, but the lack of affection and the contrast in our different values and ambitions began to weigh heavily.

The marriage was so painful that after several months, I loaded up a few possessions in my rattletrap car and left Dick and drove to Florida, where I visited a friend who gave me a parakeet in a cage. The parakeet and I went to live with Aunt Eileen and Grace and David. I got a job and considered going back to college. But I missed Dick, and I missed Doris, my surrogate mother, and I missed my hometown.

So after a few months, I gassed up the rattletrap car and drove back home to Dick, leaving the parakeet with Aunt Eileen. Other people kept giving her more birds. Eventually she became known as the Bird Woman of Seventh Terrace.

My absence had not been a wake-up call for Dick. Sharon was still a factor, and, in some ways, the hardest part was Dick's playing at being unencumbered. Then there was his obsession with speed and fast driving and racing cars, enlivened by alcoholic encounters and police at the door at least once.

He ran the roost and earned a living. I took in ironing to add to our income. When my son, Rick, was six months old, Dick vanished for three days, leaving me without a car or a telephone. After a thorough discussion of that episode, we got a phone, and he never disappeared quite that long again.

I wanted desperately to own a home, and I struggled to save money so we could buy a house, but it was an uphill fight because my husband spent every spare penny for fast cars and accessories.

We had a cheap apartment above Tribe's Tavern in Toledo, and our living-room floor was strewn month after month with auto parts. I took in other people's ironing, and I babysat.

When Rick, my first baby, was two years old, a neighbor hired me to take care of her three preschoolers, aged five, three, and two. All four children were breakfasting in the kitchen one day when I got a phone call from a girlfriend and stepped a couple of feet outside the kitchen so I could hear. It became ominously quiet in the next room. The five-year-old neighbor had discovered a new skill and somehow managed to open the refrigerator door. My little Rick grabbed an egg carton and systematically broke twelve whole raw eggs all over the kitchen table and the floor. Anyone who has ever tried to mop up one raw egg can imagine what a job I had cleaning the floor and four egg-bedecked little kids. Today it sounds like a funny scene. It wasn't then.

I pestered Dick until we bought a rundown little dump in a blue-collar neighborhood. The first night in our new home, I put my boys to bed (at that time there were two) and worked for hours to set my home in order. Then I sat and wept.

As long as we were in an apartment and just starting out, I could delude myself as to what my life was about. Now I had to consider that this was it. Somehow, I thought, I belonged in this house in this neighborhood in this world. Get used to it.

I was faced with the reality of marriage, motherhood, and a decrepit little old house that was eleven hundred square feet of shoddy construction. Downstairs, I could sit in one spot and survey the entire floor plan, which consisted of a small living room and a kitchen with eating area. Upstairs my little family slept in the two bedrooms, both of which had sloping ceilings making it impossible to stand erect anywhere but in the middle of the room. There was a small landing at the top of the stairway, which ultimately became another sleeping area under the eaves. Between the house and the garage was an attached, enclosed, unheated breezeway, which would serve as a playroom. The space between the unpainted walls and the floorboards provided an unobstructed view into the crawl space, as well as some interesting drafts.

I didn't know it that night, but six months later, the cranky old furnace would catch fire. The fire did not cause extensive damage beyond destroying the furnace, but the firemen created a number of new holes throughout the house. I will never forget the young firefighter who yelled at me to get out of the house immediately as, totally unaware of the very real danger, I carefully gathered food and clothing for my babies.

That first night, as I sat in my new home, I was more despairing than I had ever been in my life. But after making myself a cup of tea, I thought, "No, this is not where I belong. I can make a difference. I can make my life matter."

I began to create a plan. First I looked at the positives. The exterior of the little house was attractive, and the great big yard was lovely. I would enjoy the yard and fix up the house. As to the rest of my life, I knew that I had to be patient. When my boys got a little older, I would go back to school. As I examined those things that had worked for me in the past, I knew that education was the key to getting ahead, that having fun and enjoying the *now* would sustain me, and that viewing the present living arrangement as a temporary growth opportunity would provide me with a positive perspective. Life would improve. I had already learned some of the techniques of reframing (which I'll discuss at length later), so I knew how I could keep improving my performance at whatever I tried to do.

Our son David arrived when Rick was in his terrible two's. Daniel was born eleven months after David, so I had three exceptionally lively little ones at home.

My brother, David, came to live with us when he turned fifteen.

Somewhere along the way, I quit ironing for pin money and got a job at the Betty Crocker Division of General Mills, Inc.

The best thing that Dick and I managed to do was to produce our three healthy sons. Some of my insecurities from my father's desertion affected them much more than I realized. I never wanted them to think that I would leave them, and I said so often. I didn't learn until they were grown that my words were frightening, instead of reassuring.

In spite of everything, they have become fine men, and I am very proud of them.

I haven't included most of the bleak times. The greatest disappointments occurred with romantic relationships. My early abandon-ment and the sexual abuse certainly shaped my view of men and romantic love. My first marriage to my children's father was a union of two people with opposite values and conflicting goals. He was the feisty marine, home from Korea. He seemed much older than the other boys and was obviously attractive to all the girls. At first I felt that I didn't deserve his attention. Before and after we married, he spoke so scathingly of everything I did that I actually began to feel that I deserved his disdain.

It was not a good feeling. He never expressed affection, but was crushing with his criticism. He withheld sex as a means of controlling me. When I finally sought to end the marriage, I was astonished to learn that he was devastated.

In the end, all that Dick and I had in common was our three sons. I will spare you the unhappy details of the breakup of the marriage. Suffice it to say that we were divorced in 1973.

By the time of the divorce, my life was wrapped up in my sons and my work at the plant. I had been hired for the production line and then (to Dick's displeasure) was promoted to supervisor. I was the second woman at all the plants of the company to become a supervisor.

My second husband was Scott Skutt. That marriage was based on pure fantasy. The man I fell in love with did not exist. I thought that he was understanding and poetic. He was, in fact, very good looking, soft spoken, aware of world issues, and sensitive to people's feelings. What I didn't know when we married was that he was also homosexual and entirely conflicted about his sexuality.

I married Scott in 1975. Less than a year later, we were divorced, and I was saddled with a humongous debt on my credit card that Scott had incurred in extravagant gifts for me and my sons and the lavish entertainment of a homosexual lover.

The demise of this union shattered me. Not only had

I failed again, but my rival was not even another woman. As dreadful as that would have been, I knew it couldn't approach the deadly blow I suffered by losing my husband to a male. It felt as though my very womanhood had been trampled in the dust.

As outward physical evidence of my pain, I lost twenty-five pounds. When I dropped to 107 pounds, my surrogate mom, Doris, threatened me with hospitalization. My hair was drab and untrimmed, my complexion had gone sallow, and my energy level was at lowest ebb.

Scott had left in August. Six weeks later, I went for a walk and noticed that the leaves had changed and the world was aglow with amazing color. I went home and wallowed in one last purge of self-pitying tears. Then I made an appointment for a haircut and splurged on some clothes that fit.

The beauty of nature had touched me and called me back to join the living world. My sense of my human worth returned, and I reviewed my short-term relationship with Scotty from a different perspective. That was useful. I realized that I had learned a lot about myself. I knew that never again would I be so captivated that I lost my identity or sublimated my needs and ideals.

My third husband, Russ McConnell, was sixteen years my senior, and a lot of people have accused me of looking for a father. I can only tell you that I finally found a man who dearly loved and valued me and whom I respected and loved. He had a great sense of humor, danced superbly, and was always eager to frolic. He liked joking and really loved women. He was also serious and hard working, and life with him was always good and mostly fun. We were together for more than twenty years before cancer robbed me of my best friend.

It had taken two failed marriages, untold strain on my children, and disastrous consequences to my bank account before I got it right with a good, rewarding relationship with a man.

CHAPTER NINE

The Six of Us

When sister Grace was married in New York in 1975, all my brothers and sisters went to the wedding, and we have gotten together periodically ever since.

My brother Larry grew into a fine man of honor. He is an engineer and worked for the same company for years. Now that he is approaching retirement age, he is exploring other opportunities. He married a beautiful woman, and they have two sons.

Sandra came next. My father and Sally had four lovely daughters, and Sandy is the most striking of us all. In some ways, she looks less like our mother and more like Aunt Mary Louise, who mothered her after my father sent us to New York.

Sandy learned to read before she went to school. (I know because I taught her.) Aunt Mary Louise died when Sandy was in college, so she has suffered the loss of two mothers. As an adult she worked in journalism, has published several successful books, and mothered a talented and athletic son, who is now grown. Her husband, Mark, has been an environmental and business reporter and is the author of two acclaimed books.

Patricia May was Sally's fourth child. She was a very sweet, gentle girl who loved animals. She would crawl under the dining-room table with our little dog as company during her naps. She was always an obedient, compliant little girl whom adults liked. She grew into a successful adult.

Grace is a beautiful shining star. My children and grandchildren adore her. She has become a pillar of her community as a volunteer. The children who visit the library where she is the Story Lady clamor to be around her.

She has developed extraordinary skills in working with children with special needs, including autistic children. She has accomplished all this despite having to fight the demon depression – a physiological disorder that has taken down some of our greatest writers. She has a supportive, loving husband, a handsome, intelligent son who is following his dream as a teacher.

David was the baby. Our mother died when he was three. He grew up to be a sensitive, attractive young man. In his teens and twenties, he made poor decisions, but he was never malicious or mean spirited. Ultimately he married a lovely young woman, is the father of a smart, athletic, and attractive daughter, and has trained and self-educated himself as an engineer. Today he is the manufacturer's representative for one of the largest companies in North America.

I have written elsewhere in this book about the gains and triumphs in my life that my resilience techniques have earned for me.

As for all six of us, from the time my father dropped us off on various doorsteps like unwanted puppies, from Toledo to New York to Florida to Chicago, he never initiated communication with anyone. Not a single greeting card or letter or telephone call came our way, with one exception: After ignoring Larry's existence for more than twenty years, out of a clear blue sky, our father called his first son to ask if he felt that Grandpa John's modest estate had been fairly administered. During that conversation, he spoke of his "son," meaning not his boys Larry or David, but Marge's adopted child. Larry was so stunned that he couldn't say what he was thinking, "Dammit, *I'm* your son!" It was the first and last conversation between father and oldest son since the days in Toledo.

When Great-Aunt May, Grandpa John's sister, got disoriented and sick, a Detroit bank became her financial guardian. It compiled a list of her assets and sent copies to potential heirs. My father then called Aunt Eileen for the first time in decades to find out what that was about, saying that Marge told him to make the phone call. It was a terse conversation.

Over the years, he and Marge visited and called his parents from time to time. I have heard that when Grandma Lucile died, my father called Grandpa John to ask what was in her will, and when Grandpa John died, he phoned my step-grandmother to ask about will provisions.

I have never forgotten what my father did to me that awful night, but perhaps the greatest damage came from his abandoning me and my brothers and sisters.

Children are sensitive. We didn't have the maturity to say, "This is an unfeeling man. He has big problems." Rather each of us individually felt a deep sense of personal rejection. We didn't think, "He rejected all of us." We each felt, "He rejected me. What bad thing did I do? My dad didn't want me."

Today he is an old man in his nineties living in Louisiana. Only one of us ever made an attempt to communicate with him. He was unresponsive.

My Uncle Lyle considers him an unfeeling monster. After he disposed of all six of us children, he showed no interest in us. Nothing for Christmas, nothing for birthdays, nothing for illnesses, nothing for graduations. It was as though we were dead.

Poor dad. He'll never know what wonderful, bright, creative children he fathered. He'll never know what excellent, intelligent, outstanding grand-children he has missed out on.

PART THREE

Reframing for Success

The house that Karen built.

CHAPTER TEN

Capturing Resilience

I hope my history will extend your understanding of resiliency. The topic has barely been explored. Maybe it's because scientific interest is focused on specific problems and finding answers to the perennial question: "How do we fix what's wrong?"

The study of resilience examines a more positive question: "What went right?"

Throughout my years as a social worker, I have been astounded by the resilience of children. I wish we could pass it out in a capsule. As I checked the meager research, I realized that my life can illustrate how a child may grow into a competent, thriving adult after bad things happen. Children survive much worse abuse than I experienced. I've got to admit that when I read *A Boy Called It* by the very successful Dave Pelzer, which describes unspeakable abuse by his mother, I thought,

"There is adversity with a capital A. Such unrelenting, daily savagery is beyond my ken." Certainly, what I survived was more tolerable.

Many children suffer adversity and flourish more or less successfully whereas others are crushed and never recover. Why? What are the factors that contribute to resilience?

I have explored the currently emerging body of research, and I have examined my years in social work. Here's what I've learned. Here are the qualities that I found best sustained me:

- A sense of personal competence
- Consistent emotional support from one or more caring individuals
- A sense of playfulness
- A spiritual connection to something greater
- A capacity for learning and creative expression
- A willingness to work on problems with reasonable perseverance
- The ability to positively reframe

Of all of these characteristics, the ability to positively reframe or look at things from different perspectives has been the single most successful strategy for me. I want to spend much more time on the art and ability to reframe, but first let's explore the other characteristics of resilience.

CHAPTER ELEVEN

My Self Has Value

The first aid to resilience is "a sense of personal competence." How do we accomplish that? Not every therapeutic fad is helpful. Some "esteem-building methods" have included looking in the mirror and telling yourself how smart and attractive you are, chanting mantras such as "I am important," or leaving lists on the fridge crowing about your many positives.

In a 2002 syndicated column, John Rosemond, M.D., asserted that this type of "self-esteem building" produces "counterfeit positive self-assessment" that can set people up for disappoint-ment in the real world. Dr. Rosemond and I are often not on the same page, but on this issue we agree.

I don't question that it is a whole lot more productive to face the mirror and describe yourself positively than to look at your reflection and tell yourself you are fat and plain and poor. Positive thinking is good.

But I think Dr. Rosemond is right in that artificial exercises are not useful over the long haul. When I was a caseworker for a state social service agency in child welfare, it was the collective thinking that we should positively reinforce the aspirations of our foster children.

"Crystal" was a really cute kid who had been in foster care off and on for ten of her thirteen years. She had decided to become a pediatrician so she could help other kids. But Crystal's IQ was below average, and she was two years behind in school and had never successfully completed a mainstream science class. It was ludicrous to encourage her, and yet that was what was being done. Crystal could have conscientiously told her mirror how smart she was and her social worker could have reinforced this dutifully, but it simply was not constructive.

As one might expect, Crystal did not achieve her goal or even one less lofty. How much better off this girl might have been if her caseworkers had focused on recognizing her talents and encouraging her to seek success where she had a chance of finding it.

When I was in the eighth grade, Sister Mary Albertus said that I was very smart because I was a good student who consistently earned high grades. Sister was always quick to point out my academic successes. She also refused to let me bundle and band the sales-tax stamps that the class collected. She said my fine motor skills left a lot to be desired. I concluded that I was smart but inept, that I was good intellectually but challenged when faced with practical physical application. It was not a useful idea.

When I went to work in the cake factory, I wanted to be the first female supervisor. I was going to move up the ladder and increase my income while working with my mind and my influence rather than my back. But I quickly recognized that I had to achieve some basic job success to be respected by my future supervisees. So I set about learning how to run the machines and meet the production-line standards.

During my very first shift as the first woman to run the big packaging machine on the Boston Cream Cake line, I almost cut off my finger. The paper got caught in the automated feed, and I was so frustrated and so anxious to do a good job that I started the machine without getting completely clear of the cutting blade, and my little finger was sliced. My supervisor wanted me to go to the hospital, and I flat out refused. In the morning, I went to Lucille, the plant nurse, who thought stitches were probably in order. I explained to her that I couldn't fail as the first woman on the job. Lucille applied some butterfly bandages, and I returned to the line. I never became the best in the plant, but I got good enough to set a few records, and the guys respected me for how hard I tried.

With each successive machine I learned to run, each job I mastered, I became more confident. I became the first woman to supervise the manu-facturing floor. In fact, they had to change the job title, which had been "foreman" until I came along.

Ultimately I earned my undergraduate degree attending school part-time while working full-time at the plant. When I left the plant, I was the day supervisor in charge of safety and training in the packaging department. I was the chairperson of the Manufacturing Safety Committee for seven food processing plants across the nation.

I think this is a good illustration of how a sense of competency can be built on successive achievements. Valuing one's talents and personal competency are not ingredients that some guru pours into your psyche. A sense of competency is developed. It can be likened to a major construction project. The foundation has to be reinforced with the right materials, and the walls have to have the correct supports. As challenges are successfully met, confidence and ability grow.

My oldest foster daughter, Shelly, was sixteen when she came to live with us. I hadn't put up a Christmas tree for several years, but Russ insisted that we recognize having a child in our home again and put up one.

The truth is that he really liked a fresh-cut Christmas tree, and he had missed the tradition. So off he went to select the very best tree, which he hauled in and wrestled into the tree stand. It was large and grand.

Through the years, the custom in my household had been that the kids put the lights on the tree, and I'd join them for the decorating part. So I brought in the lights, untangled them, and told Shelly to put the lights on the tree and to call me when she was ready for me to help decorate. I was in the kitchen baking Christmas cookies when Shelly called me into the family room where she was working on the tree. It was a horrible scene. The lights were bunched in wads and stuck haphazardly all about the branches.

Whereupon, in my best "social worky" manner, I snarled, "Darn it, Shelly, if you didn't want to put the lights on, why didn't you just tell me?"

She didn't answer right away. Then as one lone tear slid down her cheek, she said, "They never let me decorate the tree because I'm so klutzy."

That incident taught me a lot about assumptions, expectations, instructing, guiding, listening, and more. It hurt my heart.

That first Christmas, Shelly and I took the lights off and put them back on together. We decorated the tree, and then we baked cookies. Each year, Shelly did more by herself and did it better. Today Shelly and her children decorate a beautiful tree without any help from me.

Shelly was sure she could not do anything right. When she came home from school while at her former foster home, she was not permitted to enter the house until another family member arrived. Shelly was sixteen years old and had to sit outside because she was not trusted in the house alone. It was not a question of honesty. They knew this child wouldn't take something that didn't belong to her. They simply felt she was likely to have an accident or make a mess if left on her own. Shelly had lived with these people for thirteen of her fifteen years in foster care, and they still treated her like the hyperactive toddler she had been when she first came to them. They did not value her, and she did not value herself. She had no basis for believing in her own ability.

I am very proud of Shelly. She continues to struggle with issues of confidence and competence, but she has come a long way.

You can encourage a sense of worthlessness, just as you can help cultivate knowledge of competence. Fostering resilience operates at a deep human level that includes inter-connectedness, positive role models, and opportunities for participation.

We need first to respect and respond to the humanness of all people. I have a poster that says, "He didn't look like I look or talk like I talk but when he cried he cried like I cry and when he laughed he laughed like I laugh." We are all fundamentally more alike than not.

Children need to feel that fundamental rapport of the human connection. When we live in parochial sameness, we build walls. When we label others, we show our approval of labeling.

There are powerful reasons for change.

The headlines scream of school atrocities. Parents and teachers are struggling to handle an increase in bullying among the young.

Our kids are prancing around in clothes with some designer or manufacturer's name emblazoned on their chests or backs or butts. Those are labels. Kids love them because they believe they tell everyone that they are cool, that they are affluent. Those labels are symbolic of what is going on with our young people.

By the way, I don't mean just teenagers. Look at the tots. They, too, are designer clad.

When we move from the symbolic to the cultural and societal labeling, it gets uglier because the human connection is lost. The human connection is that crack in the wall that allows us to see each person where she is. It is the oldest of the social worker's constructs. Begin where the person is. Meet our children where they are. Teach them to meet the other guy where he is. Strip the clothes of the labels, and, by the way, I would encourage a literal interpretation of that. Get rid of the designer labels. Tell your kids about other cultures, and I don't mean the sanitized popular versions. I am talking about cultural descriptions that, for example, have gone from vilifying to sanctifying the indigenous people of the United States, speech and the written word about

African Americans that oversimplify both their history and their role in today's society, and the impossibly generalized view of anybody not American as somehow inferior – all these ill equip our youth for any meaningful understanding of life beyond their own neighborhood.

Express your respect for the rights of other people and their cultural norms. We don't always have to agree, but we need to respect. Try different foods, and go to different places. Connect your children to the humanness of others.

Our children need positive role models. I am writing this at a time when the United States of America has unilaterally invaded a sovereign state on the basis of totally unsubstantiated evidence. Our financial leaders are, for very good cause, being indicted right and left for misuse of their positions. Sports and entertainment celebrities are in the headlines for drug abuse, sexual harassment, and cheating.

You could make a case for the dearth of positive role models, but you would be only partially correct. Twice a month, month after month, youngsters at a weekend retreat have been asked, as a classroom exercise, to identify the person they most respect or look up to or want to be like. It is not the president of the United States or the football quarterback or the movie star that is routinely cited. More often than not, it is mom or dad, followed by grandparents and teachers.

If you cheat on your income tax, set your radar detector so you can exceed the speed limit, take the towel from the Holiday Inn, you are being a role model. Young people have often acknowledged to me that these practices are wrong. But when I push them on it, they admit they think the mistake is in getting caught.

If you sincerely want to contribute to your child's sense of competence and resilience skills, you need to begin with your own behavior. I raised my sons during the 1960s and 70s. I remember when my Daniel confronted me about smoking. I gave him a big song and dance about adult behavior and mature physiologies. This can be an appropriate response at times. Certainly enjoying recreational sex with your spouse is, and should be, an adult activity. But smoking cigarettes is harmful to your health no matter what age you are, and I didn't tell Danny that. First I modeled an unhealthful behavior and then rationalized it in an attempt to justify my injurious habit. I didn't quit until the doctors told my mom Doris that cigarettes were killing her and my fourteen-year-old son started stealing my cigarettes. My beloved Doris, who became the mother I chose to fill the hole in my heart, died four years later, but it took Daniel twenty years to quit.

My Aunt Eileen was one of my most powerful role models. She was an independent woman with strong, unshakable ideals. My contact with her during my formative years was sporadic, but my sense of womanhood was inherently tied up with my image of her. She will always be one of the most intelligent persons I have ever known. She taught me to ask why and expect answers. She didn't preach. She practiced. That is what a role model does.

I don't think it is possible to grow in confidence and a sense of achievement without opportunities to participate. We deny people that prospect when we overprotect and overindulge them. I refer particularly to the parenting approach prevalent in American society today. Children are blatantly overindulged and flagrantly underemployed. Don't get me wrong. I am not promoting sweatshops or child labor. I mean that children are no longer considered contributing members of families. When our grandparents were parenting, the economy was largely agrarian, and all the family members, adults, oldsters, and youngsters, worked to provide for the family. In ensuing generations, the work ethic has eroded. The sense of personal entitlement that permeates today's society begins at home. Our children need to participate in the work of living.

At the shelter for runaway and homeless children, periodically we'd take in one of what my staff would call "the royalty." This was a young person who came to us alleging parental abuse, when she was, in fact, the abuser. Usually a parent woke up one morning, realized that the home was harboring a parasitic young person, and required this youngster to make some small contribution to the household. The mother might ask her daughter to clean the kitchen or some other equally odious chore. The princess then fled to our shelter. On more than one occasion, we arranged for the princess to visit our weekend attitude-adjustment retreat. Usually mom's requirements did not seem as outrageous after a weekend of classroom, exercise, and community service.

Parents of these children were grateful for whatever small improvement there was in their children's attitudes. The problem is that work is so often viewed as punishment rather than a privilege. I once visited a residential facility for adolescents that took a very different view of work. It was based much more on what the real world is like. The young residents had some basic required chores that had more to do with personal space than anything. Beds had to be made, bedrooms maintained, and laundry done. Beyond that, there was a variety of opportunity in the work life of the community. Participation earned extra privileges and money. A young person who broke rules lost the right to work. Certainly this is more like the real world where poor performance or rule breaking will result in loss of job and income.

When I speak of the opportunities to participate, I don't just mean chores at home, at school, or in the workplace. Our children need the opportunity to help provide for the greater good. Community service is more than an altruistic exercise. It is a fundamental need of humankind. We get as much as we give.

At one point, I had a Girl Scout troop of preteens. It was Christmas, and I decided that we would go Christmas caroling in the housing project that was restricted to the elderly and disabled. The area was clean, though shabby. The weather had turned brisk, and, as anyone who knows me can tell you, I am not a singer. But as we approached the first door, I began to sing, accompanied by eight reluctant backup singers.

We were embarrassingly inept, but the tiny gray-haired lady who came to the door didn't seem to notice. Tears flowed down her wrinkled face. Her tremulous voice gave expression to her gratitude for our gift of company and music. My girls came alive. They went from door to door eager to sing and laugh and talk. Not all the residents were as appreciative as the first lady, but it didn't matter. My girls knew they were giving a gift. Their sense of competency grew that day because they had the opportunity to participate.

The ability to perform effectively is developed by successive achievements. It is one source of personal resilience.

CHAPTER TWELVE

Someone in a
Child's Life

I was a lucky little girl. I had my intact family
and my mother until I was twelve years old. My
mother thought I was great. She held me and talked to
me. She told me and she told others that I was an
important, valuable person. No matter what came
later, I had my mama in my early years. The last two
years of her life, I spent a good deal of our valuable
time being mad at her. She was sick a lot, and she kept
saying she was dying. That infuriated me. She wasn't
going to die. People don't just die, and besides, none of
the adults, not even my dad, acted as if she were dying.

When she did die, I was mad as hell . . . at myself, at
my dad, at the doctors. I was moody, depressed,
and not sure how to go on living. My mother had
abandoned me.

There has been a lot of research that suggests that the early child/parent attachment predicts the quality of functioning in later life. My own history and the anecdotal evidence of my years of social work certainly corroborate the research of Drs. Erik Erikson, John Bowlby, Mary Ainsworth, Ann Masten, and Douglas Coatsworth. These represent some of the best of the body of knowledge concerning attachment and trust.

In his book, *The People of the Lie*, Dr. Scott Peck describes a disturbed child who is brought to him for therapeutic counseling. The little boy is demonstrating aberrant behaviors. When Dr. Peck attempts to work with the parents, they patiently explain that it is his job to "fix" the child, not theirs. These people were wealthy, educated professionals, and a model child was necessary to their image, but not to their lives.

The ways in which parents talk and interact with their children define what the children think about the world and themselves. These parents demonstrated zero affection and gave only marginal attention while using distinctly different words to describe their family life to the rest of the world. The disparity between reality and the parental fiction had to produce a profoundly distorted world view. The little boy was raised by paid employees, who unfortunately didn't stay long. The little boy and his parents did not continue as Dr. Peck's patients. Dr. Peck believed the mother and father were truly evil people, and I agree with him.

In some ways, their emotional abuse was more damaging than some of the overt physical abuse that I have observed. Compounding the damage, society saw these people as ideal parents, increasing the likelihood that their little boy grew up believing he had no real value. After all, he saw that his parents didn't care for him and everyone else respected them. Children need the affirmation of a parent's love and acceptance.

Now, with all that said, research also indicates that a child can increase in feelings of competency as long as there is at least one significant adult in the child's life. If Dr. Peck's little patient had had a nanny who attended to his physical and emotional needs continuously and affectionately over the long term, he may well have been a much healthier, happier child who could become a well-adjusted adult.

I was a lucky little girl. Throughout my teen years, I had not just one, but a whole convent full of remarkably strong women who cared for me and encouraged me. In general, the sisters of Notre Dame, who taught at my high school – several sisters, in particular – sustained me, encouraged me, and affirmed me.

Mary, my foster mother, barely liked me, but she provided for my basic needs and held me to high standards of social manners. I had really good friends who shared their mothers with me. Then, when I was seventeen, I found the woman who would be my second mother.

Doris Stilwell was the manager at a local drive-in

restaurant where I secured employment during my senior year in high school. Doris had two young children, but had lost three – two at birth and a son when he was two. There was a hole in her heart, and she was always mothering the teens who hung out in her store. Well, this teen had as big a need as she did, and we attached. She loved me, and I loved her.

Sometimes I might disappoint her, but I knew she would never throw me away. She was there through marriages, divorces, births, and deaths. I think some of my penchant for picking up the odd person or the lonely child was first imprinted by her example. Doris believed that we were here to help our neighbors, and, in her case, that did not mean writing a check to your favorite charity or voting for the best candidate or even being politically involved to effect positive change. For Doris, helping others was a hands-on operation.

Late one night as we approached closing time at the restaurant, my mom Doris and I talked with our one remaining customer. He was a young sailor hitchhiking home after completing his tour of duty. He was procrastinating because it was a cold winter night in Ohio, and he was reluctant to go back out into the dark and cold alone, so mom and I drove him to his home those last 100 miles.

Christy came to work at mom's restaurant when she was just out of high school. Christy was mildly retarded, but had earned a certificate of completion

---

from the local high school. Mom almost lost her job over this one of her waifs. It took phenomenal patience and much longer than usual to teach Christy how to wait on customers, clear tables, write up tickets, make change, and all the other duties of a waitress, but mom wouldn't give up, and Christy became a very competent and loyal employee. I remember Christy well because she saved her money and got her own place to live.

One day "Mister Right" walked into the restaurant. He and Christy were married with all of us attending the ceremony. They honeymooned in Michigan and tragically were killed in an automobile accident on their way home. Even as I grieved, I realized that, because of my mom, Christy had far more in her life than she ever would have had without her. And the romantic in me was so grateful that the accident happened after the honeymoon rather than before.

There is no question in my mind that a child will grow in resiliency when there is at least one caring, supportive adult in that child's life. I know I could more confidently face challenges knowing that someone thought that I could prevail.

CHAPTER THIRTEEN

Playfulness

A good sense of humor is a valuable characteristic contributing to resilience. I would expand it to what I call a sense of playfulness. It is appreciating what is funny, and it is being able to have fun. People who know how to have fun not only enjoy life more, they are better equipped to overcome adversity.

When I was a kid and my mama was alive, I played; when she died, life became a more serious matter. My ability to have fun reemerged in time.

It was an interrupted process. That first Easter without my family, when my foster brother had his new pellet gun, took aim, and fired very near me, what had begun as children's play became something very dark and different. It was very unusual for me to act out or raise my voice, especially with an adult. I think the fact that it started outside and began as play allowed me to be more open and much more vocal. What had been play became, instead, a reality check. My acting out and my foster mother's no-nonsense approach to giving comfort was the beginning of my accepting my situation. Then I began again to enjoy living. I went back outside and had fun.

At our homeless and runaway shelter, the youth and the staff were encouraged to have fun. Organized activities were built into the schedule. Staff members who retained the capacity to play always proved to be better suited to working with teenagers. Working with young people who are in crisis is a stressful and demanding job. My shelter director, Shelia Myrick, understood that the stress had to be dealt with, and she routinely incorporated playful activities into our meetings.

Have you ever noticed how often adults will resist having fun? We who played so artlessly as children decide when we mature that it is not appropriate to act silly or to laugh too loud. Just watch what happens when a group of grownups finally give in to the joy of playing. They come alive.

I was conducting a foster-parent training program, and I had grave concerns about one couple. Their demeanor was always serious, and they rarely volunteered to contribute to the discussion.

If I didn't have a sense of humor, I would never have survived.

We came to an exercise that requires the participants

to get up, move about, and get creative, and they began to have fun. Their whole demeanor changed, and they opened up to me and the rest of the group. It was as if the permission to have fun gave them permission to be themselves. Caregivers, in general, often act as if they must always present an authoritative image. I think it usually means they are afraid they will lose control.

My three sons were born within a three-year span, and my life became a blur of activity. There was never a dull moment. Very early on, the boys and I learned to have fun. I was and am a bit of a neat freak, but there was many a rainy day when our living room was a labyrinth of tunnels constructed of blankets and overturned furniture.

We walked long distances and visited every park within twenty-five miles. They've grown up liking sports as active participants, as well as dedicated fans. Daniel is totally transported by a satisfying round of golf. David and his wife, Marcie, have a beautiful home in the suburbs, and their living room is a well-appointed pool hall. If you visit Rick and my granddaughters, you'll end up playing games or jumping on the trampoline. Unfortunately, my boys also appear to be cursed with the extreme competitiveness that seems to surge through my family's genes. We are a loud, combative bunch, but we know how to have fun.

Try cultivating the ability to laugh and play just by trying it. Giggles become chortles, and chortles explode into belly laughs. Let yourself indulge in the kind of laughter that gives birth to helpless tears. Learn to dance or act or sing. Don't be afraid to be foolish. When you slip on your banana, laugh at yourself. You will be a more resilient person, and the child you teach will, too.

CHAPTER FOURTEEN

A Spiritual Connection

First of all, let's get something straight from the get-go. I am not pushing religiosity, any particular belief system, any particular denom-ination. What I am talking about is a sense that there is a greater power than oneself. Perhaps it is an all-powerful Being. Perhaps it is a strong connection to the earth and the pull of nature. Whatever that connectedness is, it will contribute greatly to your resiliency.

For me, the spiritual has more often than not been a traditional view of God and Jesus Christ. I was born and raised Roman Catholic, with all the baggage that can incur. In my young adulthood, I left the church because I got divorced, and, back then, the church of my youth rejected me for this decision. As a child, especially one abandoned by parents and family, my religion was a very sustaining force. I knew God loved me and that my mama was with God in Heaven. It seems like a very simplistic view now that I am an adult, but it was comforting and sustaining. During my estrangement from the church of my youth, I spent years looking for a spiritual home. Not until my mom Doris died did I find a place where I belonged once again.

Doris died slowly and painfully. Five months prior to her death, her husband fell to the ground and died instantly from a massive heart attack with Doris at his side. His loss was painful for her, but the revelations after his death were yet more devastating. When mom searched his papers and personal effects, she discovered that he had been engaged in a long-term affair with a much younger, singularly unattractive woman. She even found a note from this woman to papa discussing Doris's poor health and looking forward to her ultimate demise.

Five months after papa's death, I got an emergency call and hurried home to the hospital in Toledo. I was with Doris thirty-one days as they did one horrible thing to her after another, all the while telling me that she was not terminal. At the end, I threatened to harm anyone that did another thing to torment her. Her only living biological child refused to come to the hospital all the days she was there because, he said, it was too hard on him. Then he showed up at the end to demand that they continue every effort to keep her alive. Fortunately, her doctor convinced him that there was

no more to be done. She died with us all at her side.
Circumstances were such that we had to shut down
her house and get rid of all her earthly belongings
within the week following her death.

When I got home to Alabama, I was exhausted
physically and emotionally. I couldn't sleep, and I
couldn't breathe. Convinced that I was suffering
from some sort of bronchial disorder, I went to the
doctor, who sent me home with a prescription. I
took one pill. After I collapsed on the sofa for hours,
scaring my poor husband exceedingly, I looked up
the medication in my pill book. The doctor had
prescribed a psychotropic medication for anxiety. It
might have been helpful if he had explained this to
me. I took several of the pills at night over the next
few days and got myself back in hand. But there was
still an immense void.

My friend Judy Lincoln said I needed to find a church
home, and she called Rita Hayes. Rita invited me to the
Episcopal Church. It felt as if I had returned home. I
was wrapped in the old-time rituals of my youth
without the censure of Catholicism. Russ loved the little
church, and he and I joined. Churches are humanity's
creation. Jesus Christ didn't come down here and start
a building-fund drive. We humans need to have a place
and rituals and community. My relationship with God
didn't change, but I found the comfort of community.

Others find comfort outside the mainstream
orthodoxy. There is an aged professor whose

acquaintance I made through my work activities. He is a warm, sincere human being who draws his strength from a close relationship with the earth and with nature. Church, for him, is a large shade tree, under whose spreading branches he sits and meditates. My Aunt Eileen is one of the strongest advocates for true Christian values that I have ever met, and yet, she does not believe in Christianity in any way. She believes in the humanity of mankind, and she has always fought to better the human condition. Her spirituality is deep and personal.

Through the years, teens have come to the shelter professing a conviction for the Wiccan principles. I can't begin to tell you how much these declarations of personal convictions can and often do enrage the adults in the teen's life.

We long ago decided to respect the young person's personal exploration of spiritual beliefs.

Give your children and yourself the permission to explore. Watch a movie for the entertainment value, and then investigate its underbelly. Visit other religious institutions. Really read and study. Don't just read the headlines and listen to the inane sound bites that can never accurately capture the essence of any religious ideology. Be open to nature and art. The pure joy of poetry or the sheer beauty of a watercolor can lift and delight the spirit. That is spirituality.

My cousin, Laura Karasek, is one of those fey spirits that my pragmatic self can never quite understand. But it doesn't matter because she still moves me in ways that heal even when I don't understand how.

Georgia O'Keeffe wrote, "If you take a flower in your hand and really look at it, it's your world for the moment." Pick a flower and enter that world for a time. Let that world help heal your soul.

CHAPTER FIFTEEN

Learning and Creativity

Some years ago, I read that doing a crossword puzzle was like taking a pill to prevent Alzheimer's disease, and so I began working on a crossword puzzle every night. In all fairness, I have to admit that I enjoy doing the puzzles, so it is not a great chore. There is such a sense of achievement when all the little boxes are filled. Through the years, I have gotten better at filling the boxes. I learn new words, and I have to stretch to find different meanings for the clues. It is a good example of how learning and stretching your intellectual muscles can improve your confidence and faith in yourself.

An interest in learning and a capacity for creativity are factors associated with more resilient individuals. If we know that learning and creativity are characteristics of resilient people, then it follows that encouraging learning will make it more likely that a child or adult will become more resilient.

From the time I learned to read, I was a dedicated reader. My foster mother said that the house could burn down around me and I wouldn't notice until the flames licked my feet. Books have always been a refuge for me, a place to get away. They have meant enjoyment and knowledge. I learned young that knowing what you are talking about can be very powerful.

I worked with a little boy who came from a family where the written word had no respect. He was placed in a foster family whose members valued reading. They never said that he had to read, but television viewing was limited, and everyone else was reading. The foster mother made sure that there were exciting age-appropriate books available to the youngster. Eventually, he read. In the year that he remained with the foster family, his confidence grew by leaps and bounds. His ability to assess a situation and accept consequences increased significantly.

The pure joy of intellectual discovery is both rewarding and expanding. The capacity for, and connection to, learning is an endlessly valuable tool for building personal resiliency.

Creative expression is another powerful means for acquiring personal resilience. When Ginny came into the therapeutic foster care program, she had been diagnosed with multiple problems. Among them was a very low intellectual functioning. She was twelve, loving and affectionate, but unable to grasp the most undemanding tasks or straight-forward concepts. We discovered that she could learn and retain more if we used music and rhythm. Just by tapping into her creative side, she could achieve a great deal more.

One teen I worked with had a great natural talent for drawing. She used her art in her therapy to help say that which was intolerable. She used her talent to be still and hear. She gave her works to me and to others when she could not express her feelings. This creative outlet made her survival more likely. Regrettably, she was like so many of the young people I worked with – children who had been sexually exploited, raped repeatedly, burned, and battered. Her early years of abuse and neglect were so horrendous that her outlook for the future was very poor, but by tapping into her creative ability, she greatly increased her odds for success.

Sometimes we think of creativity only in terms of the arts and artistic expression through traditional art forms, but artistic expression can be found in many venues. Casey found an outlet for expressing her individuality through her dress. She was not a follower of the latest fad. She dressed herself from the time she was a little girl in her own unique style. She lived through some pretty tough times with a lot more aplomb than one would expect.

Donna was the resident who did all the other girls' hair. She braided my hair and was inordinately proud of how I looked.

Isaac taught us how to break dance, although perhaps not all that well. It is a lot harder than it looks.

Benjamin could rap. He was a poet in action. He taught me the beauty of a music style that I had summarily dismissed because of hearing some offensive professional offerings.

At our shelter, Christmas trees were trimmed, pumpkins carved, rooms decorated, greeting cards designed, kites built, and there were a myriad of other opportunities for young people to explore and grow with creative expression.

Open the door of creativity for your children. Let them mix the color palette and color outside the box. So much of our youth is spent in conforming to the rules that our creativity gets stifled. If you love to set a beautiful table and prepare a meal with eye appeal, take that extra little time to do so. It frees your creative spirit while modeling creativity in action for your children.

My Aunt Eileen enjoyed finding unique opportunities for having fun. When the children were young and at that age when they loved repetition, Eileen would tell them to get out their pencils and paper. "Why?" they'd ask. Because they were approaching the sign that said "Draw bridge," she'd explain. That little joke never failed to entertain them, and they loved having the joke sprung upon friends.

Parents often find ways of using road signs and advertisements to make travel more fun.

One sunny summer afternoon, Aunt Eileen took us on one of her famous "adventures." We went to O'Leno State Park. It is located on the banks of the scenic and unique Santa Fe River, a tributary of the Suwannee River in central Florida. Within O'Leno State Park, the Santa Fe disappears and flows underground for more than three miles before it again becomes a surface stream at the River Rise. When we entered the park, we crossed the river. We hiked through the park and arrived at the exit. Eileen asked us if we had noticed anything unusual. Intrepid outdoorsmen that we were or were not, we couldn't identify the mystery without her help. When she pointed out that we crossed the river going in but not going out, we were incredulous. We came up with all manner of preposterous reasons before hitting on the correct one. It was a great adventure, and I remember it forty years later. Eileen often made life more fun with her penchant for adventure.

I tried to follow her example when I was raising my children. And I have tried to live my life with joy and creativity. I dance in the grocery store aisles because I hear really good music streaming through the store. I wear orange shoes and red hats and pink jackets because they are fun. My granddaughter, Rachel, wore her pink boa and clear plastic slippers to the Cracker Barrel restaurant for lunch because she was a princess. My son Daniel lifts me off my feet and twirls me around every time we meet because it is fun. My granddaughter, Brittany, is one of the few remaining letter writers left in America. She hunts for special stationery and decorates with stickers and pictures because it is fun.

Don't be afraid of being different. Encourage your children to respect their own and others' uniqueness. In that very uniqueness is the creative spirit looking for release.

CHAPTER SIXTEEN

Problem Solving with Reasonable Perseverance

Early on in my social-work training, I was taught not to solve clients' problems, but to move them to find their own solutions. Have you any idea how hard it is to lead people who see no possible solution to their dilemma? It is incredibly frustrating. When history and experience have combined to convince them there is no hope, it takes prodigious efforts to change that world view.

I worked for eighteen years in a manufacturing environment, and most of those years I was a supervisor. A machine broke down, a line went down and it was my job to get it going. I had trained operators and qualified mechanics, but ultimately I was responsible for production. One night the packer at the end of the line went down. My crew had been working to repair it for more than an hour when I went to watch. After several minutes, I walked over and engaged the power button. Behold! The machine was fixed. More than likely, the mechanics had repaired the minor malfunction in the first few minutes the machine was down, but failed to perform the obvious: Once repaired, the packer needed to be restarted. I had had some outstanding training in problem solving. I wasn't trained to be a mechanic, but I was trained to look for the change.

As a social worker, I took some of this basic problem-solving training and applied it to people's problems. Often people don't know what the problem is. They know what the symptoms are, but they can't identify the underlying causes. Naturally they are not adept at solving problems, nor do they understand when to try harder and when to give up.

My sons were all toddlers when their ball rolled behind the sofa. Rick was the oldest and the strongest, and he tried unsuccessfully to move the sofa. Daniel was the youngest, and he got mad and attacked the sofa. David watched for a while, and then he crawled to the other end of the sofa where he could reach the ball. David had an innate problem-solving skill. It is a skill that contributes greatly to his resilience.

I have a friend who is bright, well educated, and determined. She can identify the problem and appropriate solutions, and she will apply all her determination toward correcting the situation. Unfortunately, she never seems to know when to quit.

Reasonable effort is not a concept that she understands. Consequently she spends considerable effort trying to fix something best left to others.

So, what are attainable problem-solving skills, and what is reasonable perseverance? The first strategy is to identify the real problem, not just the symptoms. Your trustworthy young son has without warning begun to steal money and small items from the family home. Is his larcenous behavior the problem or is something else going on? He may be doing drugs or a pastime equally dangerous. Instead of just reacting to the stealing, it is vital to get to the real issue. Then you can attack the problem with precisely the ammunition needed.

What I learned in the cake-mix factory was that the key to fixing a problem is identifying the change. If your car has operated efficiently for three years and it is stalling out now, what is the change? Sometimes to your sorrow, a day-one deviation produces a lemon. The guy on the production line made a Friday afternoon mistake, and the car has never performed at optimum efficiency. Either way, you have to trace the problem to its source.

I had a client who had been a good driver for more than a decade when she was involved in a terrible automobile accident. She recovered and went back to normal activities except for her ability to make timely decisions. Her work was suffering as well as her personal relationships. When she began looking for the change that had contributed to her indecisiveness, she realized that it led back to the accident, and she was at last able to begin to deal with it.

So you have identified the problem and the change. What now? Look for your options. The most difficult element in this process is the ability to suspend judgment as to the efficacy of each option. Wait. The more options you can identify, the more chances you have to find a fix.

I have been at many meetings where the leader says that we are going to brainstorm new ideas. There are some people that simply find it impossible to allow the unusual or outrageous idea to sit on the table without denouncing it. Everyone loves to talk about "thinking outside the box," but few of us are really any good at it.

Not too long ago, I was at a meeting with people from many different disciplines united by their interest in children's issues. When I suggested that we invite adolescents to sit at the table and participate in the conversation, I was shot down quickly and ruthlessly. One longtime educator said that she had been required to participate previously in meetings that included teenagers, and their "crazy" ideas consumed too much time. This was obviously not a group looking for original ideas or innovative thinking. I'll grant you, kids don't always understand the details or recognize the obstacles, but because of that, they often trigger new thinking even when a particular suggestion is not workable. Don't be afraid to think out of the box.

Don't be afraid of other people's opinions and ideas. You are not going to abdicate your responsibility and obligation to select an option and decide on an action, but the more input you have, the more informed can be your decision.

Don't get hung up on the idea that there is only one right way to fix the problem. I worked with a young woman who had resolved her issues of abuse by running away, and that became her answer to all her problems. What was a good choice for one issue was not the answer to every problem.

I worked with a social worker who was very good at identifying the most efficient solution, and she would focus on that remedy to the exclusion of all other ideas. The problem was that those people who were left with no ownership in the solution did not feel as compelled to see it through to successful implementation. It is sometimes better to go with the less clever solution and engage the participants than insist on the one best solution.

Now do something. If there is anything that I learned working in the cake factory, it was that it is better to do something than to do nothing. When you do nothing, a line is idle, the order is not filled, and profit is not made. When a client remains in a toxic relationship rather than doing something about it, the children are damaged even as the partners are damaged.

Keep trying as long as there is a clear likelihood for success. If you have tried repeatedly to mend a relationship and your friends or family members cling to their grievances, it may be time to say you have done the best you can and now it is their problem.

Not everyone picks up problem-solving skills as quickly as my son David, but everyone can learn to be more proficient at it. Help your children learn how by letting them work through their everyday problems rather than trying to fix every problem for them. If the solution is not the one you would most prefer but it works, let it be. Listen. Be present.

CHAPTER SEVENTEEN

Positive Reframe

The single most valuable ability that has sustained me through adversity is the ability to positively reframe the situation or behavior.

My girlfriends call me the queen of reframe. Give me a little time, and I will find a more positive viewpoint. I am trapped in a traffic jam on the expressway as the authorities work to remove a wreck. First there is a flash of irritation because I will be late getting home. Then I realize I can't do a thing about it. Finally I turn on my favorite public radio station, sit back, and enjoy the uninterrupted time.

The ability to reframe begins with looking at things from a different perspective. And that is infinitely more difficult than one might imagine. First of all, we are so influenced by what we have previously experienced that it's a terrible stretch to get past the historical perspective.

When I train foster parents, I try to explain to them the different perspective that foster children bring to their home. Children who have been in the system for a while know that the placement is predicated on their behavior. Consequently, a birth parent may well berate a misbehaving biological child with words like "not while you're under my roof" or "you'll follow my rules or you'll leave." Our birth children know that these threats are, usually, just that: threats. Foster children have experienced repeated placement disruptions for many reasons. They know they can be dismissed pretty easily. I remember a family that brought the teenaged foster child and all her possessions in the customary plastic garbage sacks, deposited her in the state agency's reception room, and departed. Her offense had to do with sexual activity with a young man of a different race in the parents' very bed.

Foster children need to hear that messing up will not buy them a pass to their next placement. They need to be threatened with words like, "You can't act up to get out. You are stuck here." Sometimes reverse treatment works better. At one residential group home for young men, the teen ran away, was picked up by a policeman, and returned to the home. The staff and other residents had a cake and a party to celebrate his safe return. In the past, every time he had gotten into trouble, he ran away and was then moved to a new placement. This time he got an entirely different perspective. He stayed after that and worked through his problems.

Learn to examine the historical perspective. Sometimes, that old perspective is very positive. Certainly, we all have had experience with the person who succeeds in the face of great obstacles. When asked how they did this, they will tell you that they did something like it before so they knew they could do it again. I read about an entrepreneur who suffered a business failure and subsequent bankruptcy. He went right back to work, saved, begged, and borrowed capital to begin over. He had built a business once, and he knew he could do it again.

The historical perspective is very powerful for good or not. Don't let the negative experience so influence you that you don't try. Capitalize on the experiences that empower you. Be deliberate, and examine the past. Too many people allow early experience to define them, to influence their performance without ever really looking at it.

How we see ourselves influences our ability to examine the situation from a different perspective and subsequently positively reframe. I worked with a young woman suffering from anorexia. She saw herself as a fat person. She spent her whole life trying to control the fat even after she was in physical distress due to her low body weight. She went into a residential program and learned to manage her fears, but she still sees herself as fat. She has never been able to alter her view of herself, even though she adheres to a plan that allows her to survive.

My mother Sally, my mom Doris, my teachers, and some early academic successes convinced me that I was a smart girl. I always approached the situation from that perspective. It meant that I could figure things out, and so I did. When I worked at the cake-mix plant, I was assigned to implement the training program for a new packaging line. Training the line crew was my assignment, but there were, initially, mechanical problems. One of them had to do with cleaning and sanitizing the line between product flavors. The only other plant using this particular equipment routinely pulled the line equipment apart to clean it. This was costly downtime and difficult work. I suggested a way to clean the system without tearing it down, a team investigated the option, tests were run, and the plan was successfully implemented. I wasn't an engineer, but, from my perspective, I was as smart as any of the other people on that team. I wasn't afraid to look at a situation from another perspective because in my view, I was capable of solving a problem.

Our ability to positively reframe is impacted greatly by how we view ourselves.

Our ability to positively reframe is also influenced by our physical and emotional health. It is certainly much more difficult to find a different perspective when we are in great pain or emotional distress. Pain can significantly cloud our judgment. One of the best examples of someone who was able to positively reframe his situation under the most adverse circumstances was a prisoner of war in Vietnam. He was imprisoned for years. In later years, after obtaining his freedom, he wrote that those years had been a powerful influence in making him the strong man that he became. He said that every day in that awful place he told himself that he was growing in power and vitality. He turned his prison into a training camp instead of a concentration camp. Despite physical hardship and emotional suffering, he successfully reframed his situation and his response to it. He was more powerful than his tormentors could ever understand.

We have observed John Walsh, the father whose child died a violent death at the hands of a dangerous criminal. He has made his entire life an example of positive reframe. His child's death is the pivotal point in a campaign to save the lives of other children. His TV program, "America's Most Wanted," has saved lives and prevented tragedies. He couldn't change the situation, but he could change his behavior.

There are two strategies for positive reframe. You can manipulate the situation. If you have lemons, make lemonade. Or you can change your behavior. If the fish are simply not biting, you use the fishing line to fly a kite.

Through the years, I have taught many classes on the art of positive reframe. I have enjoyed the responses that I get when I ask for examples of positive reframe. Some of them follow:

- an ugly girl: she's not a bit like that phony Barbie doll
- grounded for a teenage infraction: the opportunity to reconnect with my dog
- school uniforms: more clothes for dating
- wrecked dad's car: a chance to wear my cute bike shorts
- lost job: the perfect time to attend bartenders' school
- spilled bleach on favorite shirt: learned to tie-dye
- teenage parents: young empty nesters
- early male pattern baldness: save on shampoo
- early male pattern baldness: save on haircuts
- early male pattern baldness: eliminate bad hair days

People have fun looking for positive reframes to less-than-positive scenarios. They also increase their ability to positively reframe. The more you do it, the better you get at it. You have to practice.

You have to listen to your words. Negative words inhibit the ability to positively reframe. I led a workshop for a group of office workers. At the conclusion of the class, they decided to avoid negative descriptors for a week. They set up a "negativity" jar. Anyone who used a negative descriptor about another person or situation would be fined one dollar, and it would go into the jar. After two days, there were a lot of long pauses in conversations, sentences were begun but quickly aborted, and no money went into the jar. On the afternoon of the third day, the young salesman entered the office, slammed a dollar bill on the table, and said that it was worth the money to describe his unpleasant client of that morning. I will concede that the positive reframe is, on occasion, beyond the scope of the situation, but more often it is a successful strategy.

So we see that the types of words we use contribute greatly to our ability to positively reframe. We also need to listen to our bodies. When you utter a pronouncement and your stomach knots up, it is time to examine what you just said. When the hairs on the back of your neck stand up, you need to find out what is going on. Our bodies will often cue us in to that which is noxious. If your words or actions are harmful to yourself or others, it is time to weigh their value and your true intent.

My oldest son is a warrior. He is a champion of the underdog, and of truth and justice, but he sometimes has trouble figuring out what his underlying goal is. He will attack his adversary with his plethora of facts, his keen wit and satire, and his unrelenting self-righteousness. It is not a useful way of effecting change. His adrenalin is pumping, and his body is in crisis mode. If he would listen to his body signals, he would recognize that his words are not persuasive, they are, instead, weapons, and people defend against weapons. Listen to your body.

If you want to overcome adversity, the ability to positively reframe is a powerful tool. If you want to get better at it, start and then practice, practice, practice.

CHAPTER EIGHTEEN

Prescription for Personal Resilience

I have told you the story of who I am and where I am and how I got here. I told you because I thought it might help someone see how she could be successful in spite of adversity. I hoped that someone helping a young person could use it as an example of personal resilience.

I have tried to delineate some of the strategies for building resilience. They have been successful for me and for others with whom I have worked:

- A sense of personal competence
- Consistent emotional support from one or more caring adults
- A sense of playfulness
- A spiritual connection to something greater
- A capacity for learning and creative expression

- A willingness to work on problems with reasonable perseverance
- The ability to positively reframe

I believe these strategies are the icons on the screen of our lives. They help us access the program or page that will supply the data for making a good decision. I find it useful to periodically revisit my display of strategies. You may identify additional strategies that are pertinent to you. These are the everyday things we can use to overcome adversity.

The most powerful theoretical construct to impact my life was Rational Emotive Behavior Therapy as developed by Dr. Albert Ellis. My aunt worked for his institute when I was a young woman, and that is how I first became acquainted with his work. His advice is logical, practical, and doable. His words are as meaningful today as they were when I first encountered them thirty-five years ago. Find his works, and study them. They will contribute to building your capacity for resiliency.

Acknowledge your accomplishments and those of others. Recognize all the ways that have demonstrated resilience in the past. Even if you, or someone you care about or someone you are working with, is in the midst of crisis, don't get stalled there. Look back on the successes and ask, "What worked before?" and "How will what worked before help me overcome my current dilemma?"

Build on your past accomplishments, and forget about all those things you haven't yet accomplished. It is a human failing to dwell on our failures rather than our accomplishments. Get over it! What we have accomplished rather than what we have not accomplished will guide us to success. We worry about money and status, people's opinions, how fat or skinny or short we are, and many other weaknesses rather than how well we have done with what we have. I am not suggesting that we ignore real problems like cancer or alcoholism. I am encouraging you to learn from your successes and grow in resiliency.

"People are more motivated to change when their strengths are supported," deduces Dennis Saleebey, editor of *The Strengths Perspective in Social Work Practice.*

In my own practice, I worked with the mother of a teen who had just about given up on her ability to parent her child. When we began listing all the accomplishments of her child and all the strengths of their relationship, she saw how she and her daughter could reconnect. She had been so mired in the immediacy of the crisis that she couldn't stop doing what was not working and look for a new approach. It wasn't until she surveyed their accomplishments rather than their failures that she became motivated to heal the relationship and mend the family's broken circle.

Examine your strengths, and consider all those

times when you demonstrated the ability to bounce back. Build on them. Maximize your strengths and talents. Become an expert on YOU and what works for you. *You* can be resilient. *You* can bounce back from adversity to succeed.

CHAPTER NINETEEN

Prescription for Social Resilience

My plan has been to tell you about a little girl who was abandoned and abused, but grew up to be successful. My hope has been that I can share with you some strategies for you or your children or your clients that might help them achieve success. I hope that I have succeeded to some extent, but I am also compelled to talk some about sexual abuse from my experience and my social work observations and the need for reform.

Not all sex abuse perpetrators are hopelessly irredeemable. Not all perpetrators are intrinsically evil. Not all perpetrators need be discarded as human garbage. Before you get out the lynch rope or decide to drum me out of social services, please understand that I am not and will not try to justify sex abuse or alibi the behavior. What I am saying is not all sex abuse is the same and that the perpetrators are human beings. They are human beings who have done something very wrong.

Some abusers are human beings who desire sexual gratification from children rather than other adults. Sometimes they will make a relationship with an adult to hide their propensity for children; but an adult relationship is forced and unsatisfying to them. Their sexual preference is shaped early in childhood and is inalterable.

When I first emerged from graduate school, I found myself working as a therapist in a community mental health agency. A strange thing happened fairly early on, the scheduler figured out that I didn't balk at being assigned sex abuse perpetrators. Actually, I was too stupid to realize that I could be choosy or that these clients were somehow less than treatable. I just assumed that we were all there to help.

One of my first clients was a skinny little guy who could barely read and write. He had served several years in prison for rape and gotten himself into even more trouble for failing to register as a sex offender when he moved. He went to county jail for several months and was mandated to therapy as part of his parole agreement. My client was forty years old and, except for the lack of several teeth, appeared younger. After an initial session of connecting and setting boundaries, my client talked at great length about his crime. There is no doubt in my mind that he did not understand any of it.

He told me that he had been drinking a good bit and went to bed with this "good-looking gal" that he had spent the evening flirting with at a party. He woke up in the morning next to her. He said he heard someone hollering at him to open the door, and before he could get up or even cover his nakedness, the police broke down the door and threw him to the floor. It seems the girl was the fourteen-year-old daughter of a local businessman. She was hustled away, and my client was arrested. His court-appointed public defender counseled him to plead out, and he went to jail.

He took advantage of a child. He was wrong, but he still hasn't quite figured it all out.

They also assigned me one of the scariest individuals I have ever dealt with in my life. He was a short, grossly overweight man with lashless eyes. He was being investigated for abusing his two stepdaughters. At the time I saw him, he was working at a nursing home where he provided nursing care to elderly and disabled patients. I saw him two times. That was more than enough. I was physically afraid of him. He lied to me from the very first moment, never admitting to any wrongdoing, but his tone of voice and body language spoke volumes. It became paramount to me that I document our visits for the courtroom, as I was convinced that this man would be charged with sexual assault.

The next time I saw him was on the local news broadcast, which showed him chained to a water pipe in the county jail. He was too big to be put just anywhere, and he couldn't be placed in the general population, where the prisoners were outraged by his crimes. He had been arrested for abusing several elderly women and at least one man. Ultimately, the police investigation revealed a lengthy pattern of patient sexual abuse, as well as abuse of his stepdaughters.

This man was guilty of unconscionable crimes against the most vulnerable population. He is a sexual deviant who deserved to be removed from society. There is little hope for his rehabilitation. We don't know how to work with this kind of aberrant behavior, and we aren't spending a lot on research to find the answers.

Let's look at my own sexual abuse. First there was the single incident with my father. My father was an unfaithful husband. He cheated on my mother with other adult women. The night I was in his bed, he took advantage of a situation. I don't believe that he even remembers it. I've been told that he is outraged that I told anyone, now or back then, and it may well be righteous indignation because he may have blocked it. After all, it was just one time, and it was just a little fondling. (I hope my reader recognizes sarcasm.)

I have struggled with disclosing it after all these years. Why should I make my family members feel ashamed or disappointed? Wouldn't it just be easier to let that one incident in the dark remain in the dark? Probably. It is still unbelievably difficult for me to indict my own flesh and blood. In the long run, the reason that I have described that night has to do with what it set me up for later. Perhaps, without that night, I would not have been so vulnerable to subsequent abuse. I don't know, and I never will. I do know that it did not help.

In some ways, the greater damage my father inflicted was the result of his abandoning his children and lack of parental responsibility. He dropped us on various doorsteps like unwanted puppies. He never paid one penny of child support, while family members sacrificed to care for his children, and strangers provided for me. Every one of us struggled to pay for our own education. We didn't have a father sending us to college or buying our first car. Our father was raising someone else's child, his wife Marge's adopted son.

Because my father had molested me and pretended that nothing happened, I thought you were not supposed to tell, so I was an easy mark when my foster father began his long, slow grooming. The coaching for my silent compliance had begun that night in my daddy's bedroom.

After working on a very emotionally difficult case, I went to see a therapist. During our second session, I talked about my foster father and my feelings about him.

At one point, she said to me, "You have every right to be very mad at him." It was toward the end of the session, and I just withdrew. It was difficult for me because, of course, I was not mad at him. I spent the next week struggling with how I "was supposed to feel." When I went in for my next session, my therapist opened the session by apologizing. She recognized that she was mad at my foster father and had presumed that I felt the same. I have observed this behavior over and over again with many professionals. Because they find the behavior so reprehensible, because they are victims' advocates, they presume to defend the victim and vilify the perpetrator. The victims need support, and their perpetrators ought to have therapeutic intervention.

Even as I write this, I hear the hue and cry. All my friends and colleagues, who are caring and compassionate advocates, will tell you that they understand that the child still loves the perpetrator. They will tell you how hard they work to avoid vilifying the offender. I've read the manuals. I've memorized the nonleading questions and responses. It simply does not take long for the victim to understand that the perpetrator is bad. I wish I could tell you that they learn that the person they love did something wrong, but he is still a valuable, loving human being. That is not, in the main, what they hear.

Amy was seven years old when I first picked her up to take her to a therapy session. I was her transporter. She was small, with huge blue eyes and long sandy-blonde hair. She had been picked up several days earlier after disclosing to a teacher that her stepfather had been sexually abusing her. She had been placed in a well-appointed foster home in the suburbs. Amy's previous living arrangement had been with her mother, her baby brother, and her stepfather in a dilapidated two-bedroom mobile home. Amy's story is typical of how the system works.

Amy was bewildered by the whole turn of events. She had not thought that she had done anything wrong, but here she was taken from her mother and living in a very strange place, being asked questions about private stuff. As we drove back to her foster home, Amy was silent as she struggled not to let her tears fall.

I said to her, "I remember what it was like when I went to my first foster home, and it's all right to cry." That opened the floodgates. We sat together without a lot of words and cried. When her tears stopped, they were replaced with a tentative smile. My presence, my tears, her torrent of tears didn't fix her situation, but some of the hurt was abated.

It was almost seven years before I saw Amy again. I was picking up my "weekend child" from a group home and who was the newest resident but Amy? I didn't know her, but she knew me. She hugged me as if I were her best friend. Amy was a system's kid now. Amy was desperate for affection while at the same time sabotaging any placement that got too close.

Amy had very quickly decided that she was bad. After all, she was the one who lost everything. She had told her teacher about her stepfather because she had heard the "bad touch, good touch" lecture in school, and she thought the adults could make it stop. Had she fully understood the consequences of her disclosure, she might not have made it.

Her abuser was her mother's husband and the father of Amy's little brother. He did a very bad thing to Amy. The rescue system then compounded the damage.

When I was in foster care, I had a social worker who came to see me every six months or so. I had adult friends whom I trusted as well as my very close girlfriends. I could have told someone about my foster father, but I didn't know where I would go or what would happen to me, so I told no one.

Here's a different kind of case. It was my job to transport a fifteen-year-old sexual abuse victim to her appointments and her court dates. It was an unbelievable situation. The entire town was outraged at her for making accusations against her stepfather. He was a town councilman and a pillar of the community. When he had grounded her and chastised her for breaking a rule, she had disclosed his ongoing sexual abuse.

The townspeople didn't believe her. The mainstream opinion was that she was a rebellious teenager getting back at her parent. His family and friends overflowed the courthouse at every court appearance. Young people hid in the bushes and yelled at her. I listened to her, and I knew she was telling the truth.

But she buckled and recanted because the rescuing was so much worse than the abuse.

Her stepfather did a bad thing. Our culture and our judicial system make it impossible to recognize the differences in cases and work with the whole family, including the offender.

Dr. Amy Hammel-Zabin has written a dynamic book, *Conversations with a Pedophile*. She writes about a man in prison for abusing more than one thousand children in his lifetime. He has never had a relationship with an adult. He has spent his whole life abusing children with an ever increasing intensity. By his own admission, he is not able to stop the desires. By his own admission, he would reoffend if released from prison. He spent his life living without remorse, sure in his conviction that he was the victim. Only after years of therapy has he been able to recognize the harm he has done. He is not cured, and, given the opportunity, he knows that he would reoffend. He does now, at least, acknowledge that he has harmed children.

Every case is different. When we stop making blanket rules and start looking for ways to help all the parties, we will better help our children.

At one point, I almost gave up social work because I felt that my inadequate supervision had contributed to the abuse of a little girl. It was only through the counsel of my friend and mentor, Mary Groff, LCSW, that I understood that I had done the best I could in the circumstances. Mary shared her experiences from her many years as a social worker, and she connected me with other social workers who talked to me about their struggles with feeling as if they had failed. It was a difficult time, but I continued in the field and worked harder than ever for the safety of children.

The case that caused this crisis in my career was one that I had worked three years prior to leaving the state agency to go to graduate school. An eleven-year-old foster child had come from one of the most dysfunctional families I have ever worked with. The children were picked up initially for shoplifting. As it turned out, these skills were valuable in the life of this family. The children were trained and sent in to retrieve merchandise. Investigation revealed a pervasive pattern of abuse and neglect. The children were placed in foster care, but quickly sabotaged every placement. Candace was placed in a therapeutic foster home in my caseload. Because of all the family incest, I knew Candy was highly sexualized, and I set up many safeguards so the foster father would not be in a situation where Candy could for her own purposes falsely accuse him of inappropriate behavior.

After many months in the home, I let my guard down and allowed the foster father to transport the little girl from one of her many appointments to Wednesday evening church services to accommodate the family's busy schedule.

Now three years later, after being out of the home for two years, Candy had disclosed that her foster father had abused her on these occasions. No one believed it. He was such a good man. He worked so hard for the community, his church, and his family. Everyone just knew that Candy was making it up. But the allegations had to be investigated. He had to be asked.

When asked, he admitted his guilt. All he had to do was deny, and that would have closed the investigation. Instead, he told the investigator that he was so ashamed of what he had done that he had promised himself and his God that should he ever be asked, he would not lie. He said that he had never had the courage to tell on himself. After Candy left their home, he told his wife that he did not want them to foster any more girls, but he never gave her reasons, and he certainly never told her the truth. They were good foster parents to two foster sons, who were immediately removed when he admitted guilt.

Perpetrator after perpetrator never even sees a courtroom even though they are as guilty as hell. They deny and get away with it. This man admits and goes to jail. I wonder if this was truly in the best interest of society.

Mike, my foster father, came from Cumberland Gap, Kentucky. In some ways, he was the product of his environment. In Appalachia, twelve-year-old girls might become wives. At seventy-something, his daddy married his third wife, who was still a young woman, and fathered his last set of offspring. Mike, a child from his father's earlier marriage, was the first and only person in his family to earn a college diploma, and he was a successful businessman. In many respects, he was a humanitarian, but I wish he had done all he did for me without molesting me. I struggled to have healthy romantic relationships for years.

This is worth repeating: Not every child-sexual-abuse offender is beyond help. We have to treat each case on its own merits. We have to work with victims and abusers. We have to value human beings. Our job must be to reclaim all the victims.

I was at the neighborhood pharmacy one morning when Randy the pharmacist approached me with a problem. He told me that his friend, who was married to a woman with a thirteen-year-old daughter, had confided in him that the little girl had accurately accused him of sexual molestation. Before Randy uttered another word, I told him that I was a mandated reporter and would have to report if he divulged names.

Without identifying the family or, even, being too specific about their history because we lived in a very small town, Randy began to share the story. The stepdaughter had gone to her mother and disclosed that her stepfather had been touching her inappropriately for months. The mother immediately confronted her husband, who did not deny it. He did not want to lose his family, so he agreed to move out temporarily while they all sought therapy in a neighboring town. The family thought that the client-doctor privilege meant that they would be able to handle this confidentially. What happened next compounded the tragedy. The therapist said that he would see the mother and her daughter, but he didn't treat "those kinds of people." Furthermore, he was a mandated reporter, and he would be notifying the state agency.

I told Randy that the family could expect an investigator in short order. I suggested that the man continue to live separately, to avoid all face-to-face contact with his stepdaughter, to find a therapist who would work with him and a therapist who would work with his wife and daughter. I told him that the man should continue contact with his stepdaughter in the form of cards and letters. He didn't want her to feel abandoned, but he wanted the investigator to see that he was not trying to influence or coach the child in any way. I tried to help him institute things that the agency would want him to do before they asked it of him. He was not prosecuted, but the family unit did not remain intact, he lost his job, and he moved from his community of origin. Often the public backlash is more damaging than the justice system.

I challenge the prevailing thinking about pedophilia

and the penchant for grouping together all child-sexual-abuse perpetrators in one category. I challenge the helping profession to recognize the humanity of the perpetrator. I don't think it is to society's advantage to throw away human beings because they do bad things.

Let me be clear about my view of child sex abuse. I believe that it is wrong, just as I believe that any abuse of power is wrong. My fear, however, is that in Western society's Victorian view of all things sexual, the corporate reaction to child sexual abuse is not always in the best interest of the child, the family, or society.

In a well-intentioned effort to protect the young, we teach them about "good touch/bad touch." It is a mixed message. Children are sexual beings, and they fully recognize "bad touch" is in fact pleasurable.

Further confusing our children is the onslaught of media messages. In our electronic age, children are routinely exposed to implicitly sexual messages.

Many children and caregivers may take exception to my premise. They are convinced that they supervise and control what their children are exposed to. This, of course, is pure fantasy. We are surrounded and overwhelmed by media entertainment and advertising that uses sex in amazing ways to sell the marketer's product. It is so pervasive that we are almost unaware of its insidious influence.

I don't believe we will go back to a simpler time. We have to deal with life as it exists today. It is time for open and honest dialogue about human sexuality, including the twenty-first-century sexual issues of our children.

In the United States, we used to believe in something called rehabilitation. I don't know exactly when or how we moved to a mind-set of vengeance and retribution. Perhaps it began with the "war on drugs" and the "three strikes and you're out legislation." Perhaps it began because we lost our national courage and just got scared, so we started locking everyone up. Perhaps it started with movie pap like *Walking Tall* and the subsequent vigilante affronts that followed. Anecdotes suggest we now build more prison cells than family homes. Whether they are drug abusers or sex abusers, we lock people up, destroy their dignity, deny simple human comforts, and fail to make any attempt to rehabilitate them, after which we release them back into society. This policy is not working, yet in some insane reflex, we go right on doing the same things over and over again.

It is time to treat drug abuse and sexual deviant behaviors as mental health problems rather than criminal activity. It is time to start channeling some of the incredible amounts of money being spent building more prisons to providing therapy, drugs, research, residential placements, and rehabilitation for addicts of any kind. We, as a society, have to decide that all our citizens are valuable and deserve help, not just those with many resources.

Poverty has become a crime in our nation. Poor

people are looked down on and considered less than valuable, and rich people are automatically exalted. I sat next to a man at a social gathering and mentioned that I had attended a fund-raiser for the homeless in a couple's home that exceeded 25,000 square feet. I commented on how ludicrous I found this. He responded, "Those who work, get." His answer didn't make sense. The man who owned the enormous home started out with family money and made even more as a defense contractor, building weapons for killing that were produced by hard-working laborers making humble wages on the production lines.

Wealth and social standing must not be the criteria for receiving mental health services. We will become a more resilient society when all of our citizens have the opportunity to heal and improve.

Epilogue

Eileen Brand is my girlfriend, my aunt, my coauthor, and my muse. This book may well never have been written without her. Leaving my job as executive director of Tennessee Valley Family Services and striking out on my own was a momentous decision for me. I confided my fears and insecurities to Eileen, and she responded with the following letter. It is an affirmation of her indomitable spirit and an inspiration to me. I share it with you.

August 20, 2003

Dear Karen –
That was a wonderful visit. Thank you for coming. I hope it wasn't too stressful or too hard on the pocketbook for you. Thank you for bringing Judy too. I think it made it all the more fun.

I will try to make this an inspiring retirement letter.

I am proud of my United Labor Party organizational days, but I can't see any positive results other than that they enriched my mind and my life. I am proud of my kids but I'm not entering any sweepstakes for Mother of the Year, which is to say that I probably came fairly close to doing as well as I could in the circumstances, but it wasn't very good. The one thing I have spared them is that I didn't sacrifice myself so much that they feel any duty toward me beyond doing whatever they really want to do.

Looking back, I can say that life in many ways began at sixty-five. That's when I moved to Charlottesville and where I lived for almost nineteen years. It was a great place to be. I managed quite a bit of enjoyable travel in that time and built the Big House on the Hill that I'd always sort of wanted (meaning my Willow Lake townhouse), volunteered at Recording for the Blind for a couple of years (intermittent assignments), tutored individual first-graders in reading twice a week for five years, made enough impact in two years of working at a Charlottesville law firm that they invited me to firm parties and picnics for eighteen years, had some memorable Celtics parties, edited some fairly good books, and did the big nix-the-hockey-

*fields-save-the-trees crusade, organized the largest
meeting the Senior Statesmen ever had to that date
(it was "Pigs, Poultry, Pollution, and Politics" in
opposition to hog-raising and chicken-raising
factory farms), got myself elected President of the
Home Owners Association and replaced a very
poor Association manager with a good one,
campaigned for Ralph Nader and did some very
useful publicity work for his campaign, and
somehow in an anarchistic way did a lot to keep
our local book group alive and well.*

*Along the way I had the little old stroke and got
a splendid Pacemaker, but they were details.*

*And moved in year 2000 to Connecticut for a
year, back to Charlottesville for two years, plus a
move to Florida in June 2003, and a move to the
building next door October 2003.*

*However, at eighty-five I feel that the best is yet
to come if I can help you use your rich life
experience and resilient mind to produce a
blockbuster book that will change some minds and
make some social improvement, however small it
may be.*

*So, don't feel sad about no longer getting a
paycheck and being a Guntersville celebrity. Who
knows what wonders lie ahead for you?*

*Lots of love,
Aunt Eileen*

Prescription for Resilience

- A sense of personal competence
- Consistent emotional support from one or more caring adults
- A sense of playfulness
- A spiritual connection to something greater
- A capacity for learning and creative expression
- A willingness to work on problems with reasonable perseverance
- The ability to positively reframe